Dear Mr ' Willis

The life of G.W. Willis, FSA, JP

Freeman of Basingstoke
and
Founder of the Willis Museum

Derek Wren

First published 1997

Publisher by **Fisher Miller Publishing**
Wits End, 11 Ramsholt Close,
North Waltham, Basingstoke,
Hants
RG25 2DG
United Kingdom

Printed by Redwood Books

Perfect bound

ISBN 1–899077–03–0

A catalogue record for this book is available from the British Library.

Acknowledgements

Cover photograph Derek Wren, back cover photograph courtesy Graham Photography, Basingstoke (01256 782955).
Photographs A, C, D and E were supplied by the family, F is from a postcard taken by Terry Hunt, B, G and J are taken from the collection of the County Museums Service, H was lent by Eric Stokes, I and L were supplied by the Basingstoke and Deane Borough Council and the photo on page vii was almost certainly taken by a photographer from the *Hants and Berks Gazette*.

Contents

page

Acknowledgements. v

Foreword. vi

Photograph of Mr Willis. vii

The family tree ix

Basingstoke around 1900 x

The area where Mr Willis worked. xi

Introduction   The View from the Train xiii

Chapter 1 1877–1900   Growing up in Basingstoke. 1

Chapter 2 1900–1916   Head of the Family 17

Photographs. 27

Chapter 3 1916–1926   Mayor of Basingstoke 31

Chapter 4 1926–1933   Museum Curator 46

Chapter 5 1933–1940   Alderman and JP 57

Chapter 6 1940–1954   Freeman of Basingstoke. 64

Photographs. 75

Chapter 7 1954–1960   The Last Independent 79

Chapter 8 1964   The Mr Willis we knew 85

Chapter 9 1960–1970   The Last Years. 93

Poem on Mr Willis. 103

Index 104

Acknowledgements

Much of the credit for this book must go to George Willis himself. Without access to the Willis Diaries kept on microfilm at the Basingstoke Library, supplemented by similar scrapbooks of newspaper cuttings made by John Ellaway and Mr E.A. Burrows in the Willis Museum, the items kept under reference 46M90 and other material held at the Hampshire Record Office, the speeches which the *Hants & Berks Gazette* reported and the talk recorded by the Basingstoke Natural History Society this book could never have been written.

Tim Evans, the Curator of the Willis Museum, and his colleagues helped us with our searches, as did Mrs Gill Arnott and Mrs Wendy Bowen at the County Museum Services HQ at Chilcomb. I should also like to thank the staff, whose names we never knew, who assisted us at the Hampshire Record Office and the Libraries at Winchester and Basingstoke.

The Editor of *Hampshire the county magazine* gave his permission for me to quote from John Arlott's articles and the Editor of the *Gazette* has allowed me to use the vast amount of material to be found in the old numbers of the *Hants & Berks Gazette*.

I take this opportunity to thank the Friends of the Willis Museum for suggesting that I should make this study. I am very grateful to George's great-nephews and great-niece – Rowland Binns, Tony Jukes and Mrs Mary Dore – for their help and enthusiastic support.

The following all provided information: Mrs Barbara Applin, Arthur Attwood, Bob Brown, 'Mac' Capelin, Ian Carey, Ken Chapman, Maurice Chapman, Max Deadman, Miss Mary Felgate, Mrs Nora Goddard, Mrs Jean Holton, Mrs Pat Holton, Mrs Nora Jupe, Mrs Beryl Kay, Derrick Mant, Mrs Barbara McKenzie, Cllr Dudley Keep, 'Ernie' Major, Mrs Mary Oliver, David Pettle, the Misses Pink, Mrs Margaret Rea, Philip Rope, Mrs 'Debbie' Reavell, Miss Margaret Sadler, Brian Spicer, Eric Stokes, John and Hazel Sweetman, Miss Hilda Wood and Miss Kathleen Wornham as well as the Superintendent Registrar of Basingstoke, the National Motorcycle Museum, the Automobile Association, the Society of Antiquaries of London and the Antiquarian Horological Society.

David Mann created the maps and our son John solved the technical problems caused by my ignorance of word processors.

I owe a great deal to Fisher-Miller for their wise advice in the stages of preparing the material for printing, and lastly I would like to thank my wife Margaret who has been my constant companion on this voyage of discovery.

Foreword

It gives me great pleasure to commend this delightful book to you. It has been painstakingly put together and well researched by Derek Wren, ably assisted by his wife Margaret.

George Willis was unquestionably one of the most outstanding personalities and benefactors of Basingstoke in this or any other century. His contribution to the town and the countryside around, that he loved so much, is incalculable. He was multi-talented as an historian, archaeologist and naturalist, as well as a skilled horologist.

The esteem in which he was held ensured that he became the first Freeman of the Borough and had the Museum named after him.

I did have the pleasure to follow in a very minor way, the same path in life as George, being educated at Queen Mary's Grammar School and later being a governor of the school, as well as serving as a councillor and mayor. I therefore know the highs and lows he would have experienced.

The man with the sprightly walk, sharp no-nonsense responses, with a deep affection for his town and fellow citizens, left an indelible mark on me and I am sure many others.

I fear we will never see his like again.

Dudley A. Keep
President
Friends of the Willis Museum

1960 *George Willis in his shop using a watchmaker's glass (82)*

The Willis Family Tree

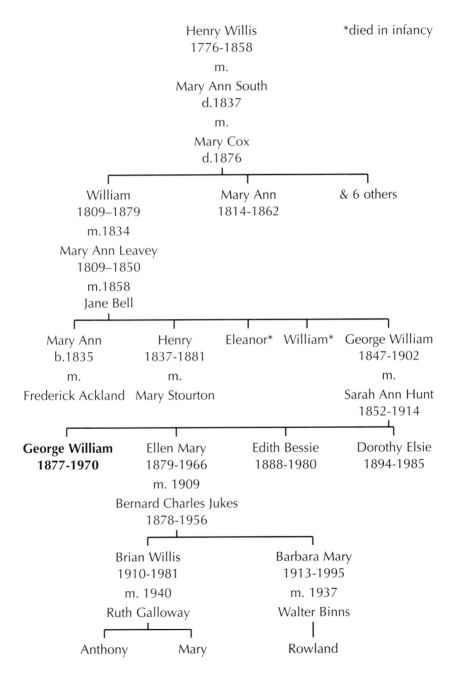

Henry Willis
1776-1858

m.

Mary Ann South
d.1837

m.

Mary Cox
d.1876

*died in infancy

William
1809–1879
m.1834
Mary Ann Leavey
1809–1850
m.1858
Jane Bell

Mary Ann
1814-1862

& 6 others

Mary Ann
b.1835
m.
Frederick Ackland

Henry
1837-1881
m.
Mary Stourton

Eleanor*

William*

George William
1847-1902
m.
Sarah Ann Hunt
1852-1914

**George William
1877-1970**

Ellen Mary
1879-1966
m. 1909
Bernard Charles Jukes
1878-1956

Edith Bessie
1888-1980

Dorothy Elsie
1894-1985

Brian Willis
1910-1981
m. 1940
Ruth Galloway

Barbara Mary
1913-1995
m. 1937
Walter Binns

Anthony

Mary

Rowland

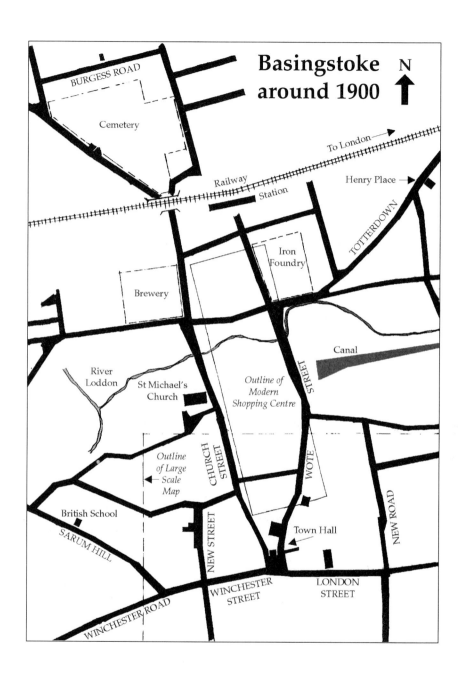

Reproduced from the 1940 Ordnance Survey Map

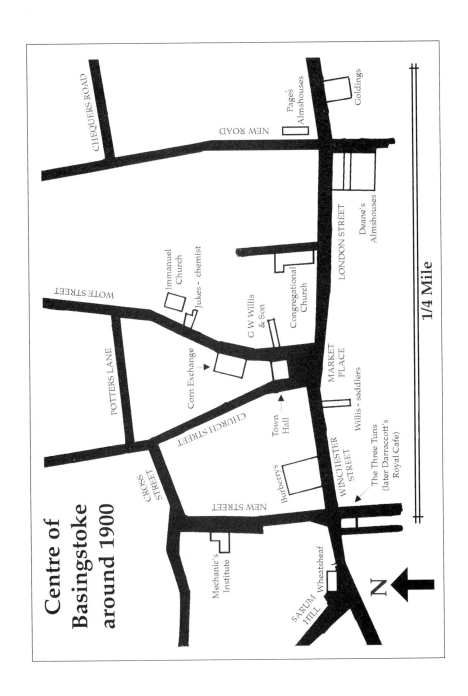

Centre of Basingstoke around 1900

CHEQUERS ROAD

NEW ROAD

WOTE STREET

POTTERS LANE

CROSS STREET

CHURCH STREET

NEW STREET

Immanuel Church

Jukes - chemist

Corn Exchange

G W Willis & Son

Congregational Church

LONDON STREET

Pages' Almshouses

Goldings

Deane's Almshouses

MARKET PLACE

Town Hall

Willis - saddlers

Burberry's

WINCHESTER STREET

The Three Tuns (later Darracott's Royal Cafe)

Mechanic's Institute

SARUM HILL

Wheatsheaf

N

1/4 Mile

Reproduced from the 1940 Ordnance Survey Map

Introduction
The View from the Train

If you are travelling from Southampton to London by train, look out to your left as you come into Basingstoke and you will just get a glimpse of the cemetery lodge where John Arlott, cricket commentator and writer, was born in 1910. As the train leaves the station it is no use looking out on the other side for Henry Place where George William Willis, Freeman of Basingstoke and founder of the Willis Museum, was born in 1877. The site is somewhere underneath the road which leads to the line of multi-storey office blocks known as Basing View.

John Arlott and George Willis were the outstanding Basingstokers of this century; the one famous all round the world: the other little known outside his home town. At different times, in 1964, my wife and I had the good fortune to meet them. They each, on separate occasions, came to our home. We only saw them a few times after that year but our memories of them are as vivid as ever.

Although separated by an age difference of thirty-two years, they each respected and admired the other. They were both old boys of Basingstoke's Queen Mary's School, having got there by winning the Aldworth Foundation Scholarship. They were self-educated after leaving school. They shared a love of their home town. Both had an enormous capacity for work. Both were avid collectors. Yet no two people could differ more in their personalities and in the pattern of their lives.

More than thirty years later the contrast between their characters still intrigued me. I offered to speak about them to 'The Friends of the Willis Museum', to leave my mind clear for other interests. While preparing for this talk I read John Arlott's own *Basingstoke Boy*, Timothy Arlott's life of his father and the official biography of John Arlott by David Allen. Without sharing the obsession so many of our friends have for the game of cricket, I felt I knew John Arlott. But Mr Willis – I always knew he was George only to his parents and sisters – remained an enigma. Where had he come from? What events shaped his life? What sort of a person was he, away from his shop, the Council chamber and his museum?

When I gave my talk the contributions of the audience only brought home to me how many questions remained unanswered. Margaret and I decided to find out whether these questions could be answered. The quantity of material kept in the Hampshire Record Office at Winchester, the Basingstoke Library, the Willis Museum and in people's memories amazed us. Every day we found new pieces of this giant jigsaw, although we knew the picture would never be complete.

After George Willis had been made the first Freeman of Basingstoke, his sister Edith asked him, 'Are you going to write some memoirs and reminiscences, some day?' Apart from countless articles in the local paper and talks to different societies, he never wrote the book his friends were waiting for. I hope that this biography, in which, inevitably, I have sometimes had to draw conclusions based on conjecture rather than fact, will go some way to fill that gap.

Derek Wren
Basingstoke
September 1997

Dear Mr Willis

Chapter One
1877–1900 Growing up in Basingstoke

'I was a very shy, difficult and reserved boy ...'

The battle of Waterloo was still a year away when, in 1814, George's great-grandfather Henry Willis became the owner of a saddlery and harness-making business in Winchester Street, Basingstoke, in a position not far from the Town Hall. The stagecoaches, which linked London with the west country and which always stopped in Basingstoke, passed his door.

Henry was born in 1776 at Hartley Row, a small village on the London road, some five miles from Basingstoke. An account in the family records describes how as a youth he:

> ... *followed the plough; became a soldier; saved money; apprenticed himself to a Harness Maker at Hartley Row. Worked for Mr Rogers, Harness Maker, Basingstoke, lodging at Mr W'm Smith's in Wote Street and walking home to Hartley Row every Saturday and returning to his work again on Monday morning, until Mr Rogers became bankrupt, when he purchased his late master's premises in Winchester Street and took possession April 6th 1814.*

He was also Drill Sergeant in the Yeomanry for many years, which appointment he resigned in 1832. It is a classic story of a country boy making good which, if it weren't true, might have come from a novel by Thomas Hardy.

Henry had married Mary Ann South, a girl from his home village, who bore him eight children, of whom only two survived him. Mary Ann died at the beginning of 1837. The following year Henry married Mary Cox and then the next year he retired to live in Rose Cottage, the home he had built for himself at the rear of the business premises. He handed the business over to his son William.

Before joining his father in the firm, William, who was the grandfather of our Mr Willis, had worked in Winchester. The year 1839 was not an auspicious year to become the owner of a saddlery business in Basingstoke. It was the year when the stagecoaches ceased to run. The railways had, presumably, put them out of business. Although this source of work had gone, the firm of William Willis managed to thrive. It won a Bronze Medal and Certificate at Reading in 1865. Lord Bolton was one of the customers.

William's first wife was Mary Ann Leavey. The couple had five children, two of whom died in an epidemic of scarlet fever in 1846. The last child, George William, was born the following year. His mother died when he was three years old. For several years William's sister, another Mary Ann, lived with them until William remarried.

Henry, William's elder son, joined the business but George William, who was George's father, had no desire to work with leather and horses. Perhaps he saw that the firm could not support him and his brother. He tried his hand at teaching, and then became apprenticed to Frederick Lodder who was a watchmaker and jeweller with a shop a short distance along Winchester Street from the saddlery.

While learning the skills of a watchmaker and jeweller, George the elder was also becoming involved in the life of the parish church. For a short time he was one of two men acting as physical training instructors in the timber-framed room, now known as 'the Barn'. This had been a malthouse, forming part of the the building built, at intervals, over several centuries, not far from the parish church, which has the curiously inappropriate name of 'Church Cottage'. Later he became Superintendent of St Michael's Boys' Sunday School, secretary of the local branch of the Church of England Temperance Society, and took his turn in preaching at the mission hall the Church had established at Totterdown in the Reading road, just a little way south of Henry Place. This mission hall was also used as a 'Day School'.

George Willis the elder was twenty-seven when, in April 1875, he married Sarah Ann Hunt. Both Sarah's parents had probably died before she married. Her father, who was a farm worker, certainly had. When Sarah was born her mother marked the birth certificate with a cross. Sarah was more fortunate. In the 1871 census, when she and her younger brother were living in the Reading road, she is described as a pupil teacher. I am reasonably certain she was teaching in the Church of England school where George Willis preached in the evenings. There is a photograph in the Willis Museum, which I believe is the one referred to in a letter I received in 1970 from a 90-year-old lady, who told me she had been in Sunday school with George Willis (the younger), and had given the Museum a 'photograph of us school children at the small school then called Totterdown in the Reading road, opposite the Salvation Army Temple'. On the back of this photograph, which shows two teachers and children in front of a Victorian school building, is written 'Miss S. Hunt who later became Mrs G.W. Willis'.

Perhaps George and Sarah met at the mission centre. They were married at St Michael's Church by the vicar, the learned, austere Canon

Millard. Sarah was twenty-two when they married. If she was as good looking as her daughters were to be, she must have been quite a beauty.

A month after the wedding, Sarah was appointed to act as a Junior Mission Woman in the parish. The terms of her appointment, handwritten and signed by the vicar, are kept at the Winchester Record Office. They are clear and precise. She was to visit and read in the districts assigned to her on four days of the week, viz: Tuesday, Wednesday, Thursday and Friday, and for three hours of each of these days. She had to keep a 'Log Book' and to submit it to the vicar's inspection weekly, also to make out a 'List of the Poor' in each of her districts. Sarah's districts covered eight roads, ranging from the Reading Road, where she was living, to the Cliddesden Road on the the southern, opposite, side of town. These ladies were sometimes known as 'Bible Women' because they went from home to home reading the Bible. Sarah was paid for this work eight shillings (40p) a week.

Many of the homes which she visited and, indeed, the home she had grown up in with her father, mother and three brothers, were in a different world to that of the vicar. Her home had been a cottage in Gas House Lane, with the gasworks at the end of the road. The spacious Georgian vicarage was set in several acres, gardens which now form a small public park. The 1871 census shows that the staff at the vicarage consisted of a footman, cook, housekeeper and nurse. This was at the time when *Kelly's Directories* divided the population into three categories – the gentry, tradespeople and the rest. The latter, the largest group, were not listed but the clergy shared a place with the gentry.

We found only one map showing Henry Place, where George William Willis was born on 13 October 1877, and where his parents probably lived for the first few years of their marriage. This is the map prepared By Lieutenant L. Ferrier RE in 1872, marked to show new sewers that were to be built. Henry Place was at the north-east corner of Basingstoke. Only the *Castle Inn*, which was on the other side of the road, and the railway lines, which run behind the pub, still exist. This public house was one of the taverns which encircled the town, offering liquid refreshment for farmers as they came in from the country, and the last chance to have one for the road as they went home.

Although the name has disappeared, a photograph of the Reading Road, taken before the area was cleared for town expansion, shows a group of terraced houses – possibly three, with a common forecourt on the north side – one of which was, I believe, the Willis home. There were open fields to the west but the workhouse could be seen in the distance. Just to the south were the gasworks. Situated where, according to the wind direction, you breathed in either the fumes from the gasworks or the soot-laden smoke from the trains, it was not, I imagine, a home which George's parents had chosen because of its desirability.

The standard of life at Henry Place was probably fairly basic but my guess is that George and Sarah were, like George's grandfather at the beginning of the century, saving for the day when they could enjoy the independence of George starting in business on his own. He did this, in 1878, in premises at the bottom of Wote Street. Two years earlier his father had handed the saddlery business over to George's brother, Henry. Then early in the summer of 1879 William's second wife died. William made a new will in which he left the bulk of his estate to his son George, having, as he said, already provided for Henry. There was also an allowance for his daughter Mary Ann who was married to Frederick Ackland, a manufacturer of boots in Bristol. Six weeks after his wife's death, William died. Later in the summer, to quote from the family records, the saddlery business 'came to an untimely end'.

The premises were sold the following year when, on Thursday 11 March 1880, at two for three o'clock in the afternoon, an auction was held at the *Wheatsheaf* Hotel in Basingstoke to sell the freehold house and shop and extensive premises, and including fixtures, in the High Street (now known as Winchester Street) 'where for the last 60 years the well-known family of Willis successfully carried on a first-class trade as Saddlers and Harness Makers'. The notice of the auction describes the property as having a frontage to the High Street of about 22 feet (7 m) and a depth of about 250 feet (76 m), and goes on to say that 'the situation being next the Capital and Counties' Bank, in the very centre of the Town, with a capital frontage, offers the opportunity (rarely occurring in this flourishing Town) of securing Premises suitable for any business'.

Fortunately for William's son George, after having inherited his father's estate, suitable premises for his business became available at the top of Wote Street at the other corner of the Market Place from 15 Winchester Street where the saddlers' business had been carried on and where he had lived until he married. The premises he bought had been the *Fox and Hounds*, known as a popular tavern, until it closed down. In May 1881 the local newspaper, the *Hants & Berks Gazette*, in an article reporting on the vast alterations and improvements that had been made in the street property of Basingstoke during the last few years, noted that 'The *Fox and Hounds* public house has vanished from this street, and in its place we have a shop which will be opened shortly by Mr Willis, jeweller.'

George and Sarah had already moved out of Henry Place, and were living in Rose Cottage, the home that grandfather Henry had built for himself. The 1881 census shows that they then had a fourteen-year-old girl living with them. Her duties as servant probably included, as well as general housework, looking after the two children, a son, aged three, who had been given the same names, George William, as his father and a daughter Ellen Mary, who was one. When Mr Willis moved his business to 2 – now numbered 3 – Wote Street the family moved as well and lived in the two storeys above the shop.

From being on the edge of town they were now at its centre, joining the community of tradespeople who, then and for many years to come, virtually ran the town. The shop looked out on to the side of the Town Hall. Market Place, in front of the the Town Hall, formed the hub of Basingstoke. Here four streets meet. London Street and Winchester Street, going east and west from Market Place, were on the direct route from London to Winchester, Salisbury and beyond. There was less traffic now that most people were taking the train for longer journeys. Young George was probably unaware of his changed situation. When, in the 1950s and 1960s, George described the town that he grew up in, he remembered it as 'a very settled place, a place where you knew almost everyone you passed in the street'.

In the fairly small area covered by the streets which radiated from the Town Hall most people probably did know each other. Many businesses had been established for two or more generations. The families lived over the shop. The children went to the same schools. Everyone walked about the streets as they do again now in this part of the town. There was time then to stop and talk, which friends can't now do when they pass each other in their cars. Probably farmers and people who came in to Basingstoke regularly from the countryside became equally familiar. Between 1871 and 1881 the population had grown from 5574 to 6681, so a good many strangers must also have been seen about.

As George grew up he had advantages which young people today have lost. Once he was able to run about he may have been allowed to wander the streets where he and all the other children in the district were well known. His world combined the excitement of the town, and the varied activities to be seen in the Market Place, with the peace and beauty of the countryside which George was to say, in later life, was only five minutes' walk away. Early in 1997 I walked, in less than twenty minutes, from the *White Hart Inn* which was then the first building you met, coming from London, to the *Wheatsheaf* where the road divided, one branch going to Southampton and the other to Salisbury. Here open country was just down the road.

In a talk, given to the Basingstoke Natural History Society in 1963, George has left us a detailed description of the Basingstoke he knew as a boy. He remembered not only the sights but also the sounds, in particular the noise which the iron tyres, fitted to the wooden wheels of the carts, made as they rattled over the rough flints with which the the roads were made. These flints were extremely dusty in dry weather so water carts were used, great tanks with a spray on the back, which periodically paraded the town and converted the dust into mud. Before tarmacadam was introduced, the council tried laying wood blocks in the Market Place but after rain the blocks swelled and came up.

George went on to tell of the street lighting of the time which at first was by provided by burning gas as a naked flame in lamps on metal standards or fixed to the corners of buildings. Later these were replaced by incandescent gas lighting. The lamplighter who came round every evening was one of the characters of the town. Others were the muffin man, wearing a beige apron with a tray of muffins on his head, the milkman, who filled housewives' jugs with a measure from an open bucket, and the butcher who carried meat round, exposed to the air.

Every Wednesday and Saturday, stalls were set up in the Market Place for the weekly markets, as they still are today, and as they have been since before 1214, the year when, by royal command, the day for the market was changed from Monday to Wednesday. After the grain had been harvested farmers brought their samples in on Wednesday to sell their crop at the Corn Exchange, now the Haymarket Theatre, which is just a short distance down the road, on the other side of Wote Street. On these days it was hardly possible to get down Wote Street because of the numbers of horses waiting to take the farmers home. The public houses were enjoying the best trade of the week.

Another link between Basingstoke and the surrounding countryside was the annual Michaelmas Fair, held at that time at the top of Sarum Hill. As well as the excitement and noise of the roundabouts and the steam organs, George remembered farm labourers standing in a line along the road, waiting to be hired by a farmer for the following year. Shepherds were distinguished by a piece of wool, ploughmen by corn and the men who looked after the horses by a length of whipcord. After being engaged they were paid £4 to cover their expenses in moving to a different farm. Some of this money was spent shopping in the town, one shop providing free meals for customers. In the Market Place at Michaelmas boxing booths were set up where itinerant professional boxers challenged the farm workers. As George remembered those occasions it was the farm workers who always came off worst. At least it was less cruel than in earlier times in the century, as remembered by George Woodman, the Odiham chemist, when a bear was brought out for baiting by dogs. This was kept down what was then known as Bear Alley, later renamed Caston's Alley. Today walking through Caston's Alley is the quickest way to get from the short-term car park to McDonald's. Some days a one-man band comes through the Market Place and a few years ago my wife and I saw Morris Men performing but it must have been a more lively, even – at times – violent place during the last century.

George did have one memory of seeing a bear, which he was fond of recalling. This was a rather shabby bear, being led by an Italian along a road at the edge of the town. What puzzled George was that cows in the adjoining field rushed to the hedge, with their tails stretched out horizontally behind them, watching the bear in an apparent state of fear. What primitive instinct, George asked, caused the cows to react in this way on seeing this strange animal for the first time?

Long before George's encounter with the bear, his mother and father had suffered a major upheaval in their religious life. Rumour has it that Sarah had a disagreement with the vicar. If this is true, she was not the first nor the last person to have this experience. Whatever the reason, around 1885, George's parents ceased to worship at the parish church and transferred their allegiance to the Immanuel Church, just a short distance down Wote Street. This church belonged to the Countess of Huntingdon's Connexion. Although the Countess had founded this sect in support of the Wesleys a hundred years earlier, the Immanuel Church in Basingstoke was bound by its deeds to use the Liturgy of the Church of England for divine service. It also had a good reputation for its music, with an organ, said to be a fine instrument but too large for the church. The Willis family must soon have felt at home there.

By this time George had started school. In his talk to the Basingstoke Natural History Society he said that his first school was the British School in Sarum Hill, but this seems unlikely. There were two schools he could possibly have attended when he reached the age of five or six. One was the National School, supported by the Church of England, and the other was the British School which, in his own words, catered for 'non-adherents to the Anglican faith'. Would he have gone there when his parents were attending the Anglican church, or did his education not start until he was nearly eight years old? My wife and I both have a memory of Mr Willis telling us that he once attended the National School for infants, held in a room at Church Cottage. We also have a distant memory of his telling us how they sharpened their pencils on the brickwork outside. The grooves that the children made in the brickwork can still be seen, but we have found no evidence to confirm that George was one of these children.

I still, however, believe that he first attended the National School, and that he would have been taken away and sent to the British School when his parents ceased to attend St Michael's Church. The British School was in Sarum Hill, then called Salisbury Street, just beyond the *Wheatsheaf*. This had been opened in 1840, and extended in 1875. The foundation stone of the 1875 building had been laid by Richard Wallis, a Quaker who had been mayor in 1863–4. He was an active reformer who had ignored the criticism of those who opposed it on the ground that 'it was not right to teach poor children so much; when they grow up we shall get no work out of them'.

George Willis said very little about his early school days. He remembered the British School as a place where he was uncomfortably cold – the room that he was in being warmed by a single gas fire, which gave very little heat at all. Each week the children took their contribution to the school's income. This varied from 2d to 4d (1–2p) a week, the children being assessed on their parents' income. Throughout the 1880s the number of children attending school rose all over the country, as the 1870 Education Act took effect. In Basingstoke the numbers rose to nearly 400 at the British School and 800 at the National Schools. Representation was made to the Town Council on behalf of both schools. The Council accepted its responsibility. A School Board, with seven members elected by the town's ratepayers, was appointed to organise the building of Basingstoke's first Board School. They chose a site where sheep fairs had been held after the Enclosure Act, on high ground which was considered healthy for children. George Willis's first day at the new school, later to be named Fairfields, was the day it was first opened – 16 February 1888. Many years later he wrote,

> I was present at the official opening of the new Board School, as a member of a class deputed to sing a song at the appropriate period in the programme. As this involved sitting quietly during all the other items of a long afternoon, which to us consisted of a dull, unintelligible mumbling from the main hall, I can still feel the boredom I suffered during that day's proceedings.

Unbeknown to George, the party of distinguished citizens who, as he took his place, were probably still finishing the lunch they were enjoying at the Town Hall before proceeding to the new school, included at least two persons whose achievements he would emulate in his own life. One was the vicar, Canon Millard, who – together with antiquarian Mr Baigent – had written a history of Basingstoke which, if you are lucky enough to find a copy of this valuable book, is still the best general account of the town's history. The other was Richard Wallis, the former mayor, who had worked tirelessly for improvements to the town's sanitation as well as its education facilities. His brother Arthur founded the firm of Wallis and Steevens, makers of road rollers and one of the town's largest employers.

To return to the Town Hall, the principal speeches were given after the mayor's luncheon, before the party left. The mayor, Thomas Maton Kingdon, said, in defence of the expenditure of money which the building of the school had incurred, that the school 'ought to reduce their poor rates, to help in their local government and to lessen the number of their criminal classes'. Alderman Wallis also spoke in favour of the usefulness of education.

At 3 o'clock the party left the Town Hall to join the procession, led by the band of K Company, Hampshire Rifle Volunteers, followed by the Fire Brigade, Borough Police and just about anybody who had any position in the town, with visitors and ratepayers bringing up the rear. Having arrived at the new school, there was an inspection of the building with openings of main doors with silver keys, followed by more speeches and finally the singing of the National Anthem. No wonder it had seemed a long, boring day to ten-year-old George Willis.

What little we know of the two years he spent at Fairfields is insufficient to judge whether he continued to find his days there boring. When reviewing a book written by his friend Stephen Usherwood, Mr Willis wrote, 'some of us have the dreariest memories of our school history lessons owing to the stodgy character of the history books of our earliest time'. Does this refer to his two years at Fairfields? George Gage, who had been headmaster at the British School, became headmaster at Fairfields when the new school opened. He was faced with what today would be considered an impossible task. In its second year there were three classes in the Boys' School which contained 92, 77 and 78 boys! It is possible that the Monitoring Method of teaching was used. If this was the case, each class would have been divided into groups, the brightest boy in each group selected to be taught by the teacher. That boy would then return to teach his group. Whatever the method used, when George Willis took the examination for the Aldworth Foundation Scholarship which would earn him a place at Queen Mary's School, he was not only one of the six successful candidates, but came first in both the religious and secular parts of the examination. He was one of the first of many men and women, successful in later life, who were educated at Fairfields.

Meanwhile his father was succeeding in building up his business as watchmaker and jeweller, despite the competition in the town. There had been a watchmaker and jeweller's shop owned by a member of the Gregory family in Winchester Street, just along from where Willis, saddler had his premises, since the early part of the century. The Gregorys also sold or hired out pianos. Frederick Lodder, to whom George Willis senior had been apprenticed, was still in Winchester Street, and, in 1883, Charles Porter, member of a well known firm of watchmakers, had opened a shop in Church Street.

When, in 1887, the tower on the roof of the Town Hall was extended and a new clock installed to celebrate Queen Victoria's Golden Jubilee, all paid for by the brewer Colonel John May, it was George Willis who won the contract to install the clock. Young George, who had gone up on the roof when his father was working there, was one of the many small boys in the crowd in the Market Place on 28 June 1887 watching to see the Hon. Diana Sclater Booth unveil the clock, in the presence of Lord Basing. The boys were highly amused when the tarpaulins failed to part and the workmen had to do the job. The character of the ceremony was captured perfectly by the official photographer in a photograph now displayed in the Willis Museum. This shows the distinguished guests seated on a line of chairs across the square, some of the men wearing aldermanic robes, all wearing top hats, and the ladies in long dresses. Behind them, standing up, are the middle classes in their bowler hats and to the right of the picture, with a policeman keeping control, are the lower orders wearing caps and other headgear. In this society, where everyone knew their place and, on grand occasions, wore a hat to show what it was, where should we look for George's father? Was he one of the men wearing bowler hats?

His ability had certainly been recognised by then at the Immanuel Church. A year after joining the church he was elected both secretary and superintendent of the Sunday School. An article on the history of the Immanuel Church, published in the July 1895 issue of *The Harbinger* speaks of the 'devoted labours of the energetic secretary Mr Willis'. Another position he held was as treasurer of the Society for the Spread of the Gospel at Home and Abroad. 'Abroad' for the Countess of Huntingdon's Connexion meant Sierra Leone. It still supports mission churches in that part of Africa.

There is no mention of Sarah taking an active role in the Church. She was no doubt fully occupied in running the home. The census of 1891, the last year for which the details have been made available to the public, describes the Willis household, all living in the two floors above the shop. It consisted of George William and Sarah Ann, their son George, now thirteen years old and a scholar, his sister Ellen Mary who was eleven, and the youngest girl Edith Bessie, who was only two. Also in the home lived Emily Perkins, 25, who worked in the shop as a jewellery assistant and Jane Cooper, 21, who was a domestic servant. Emily had been born in Marylebone, so people were coming out from London to look for work in Basingstoke more than a hundred years ago. Jane had come in from the village of Whitchurch. The girl who had been working for them ten years earlier had moved elsewhere.

It was, no doubt, a contented household, fairly prosperous, industrious and serious. One can imagine the pleasure with which George and Sarah read their son's school reports, after he had moved to Queen Mary's School, by the light of an oil lamp, in the evening after the shop was closed. He was reaping the benefit of being in small classes and the high standards the school maintained. The reports for the Easter and Summer terms for 1891 survive. In the Easter term George was fifth in English grammar, and third in mathematics but first in the other subjects – general knowledge, Latin and French. His drawing was very good. The masters wrote that his work was very good. His conduct was very satisfactory. He was never late, never absent.

Speaking at the ceremony to make him a Freeman of Basingstoke, Mr Willis said,

> I am delighted to pay tribute to my school days at Queen Mary's School where the seeds of many branches of my interests were sown. I recall the names of Chadwick, Phillpott and Caldicott. Some of the seeds lay dormant for a long time and after forty years I was surprised when presented with the problem of deciphering ancient local documents the seeds of my Latin seemed to sprout again.

His love of history was, I am sure, one of the interests which developed from attending an ancient grammar school which could trace its roots back to the sixteenth century. This was when the Guild of the Holy Ghost was re-founded by Mary Tudor, with a priest appointed whose duties included the education and instruction of the young men and boys of the town as well as the performance of Divine Service.

In 1856 the boys of Queen Mary's School had moved from the timber-framed room, built on to the ruins of the Holy Ghost Chapel when the Guild was reformed, to a purpose-built school in the Worting Road, some distance beyond the first school George had attended in Sarum Hill. The west wall of the Holy Ghost Chapel and the walls and tower of the adjoining Chapel of the Holy Trinity can easily be seen from the train on the east side of the cemetery lodge where John Arlott was born. The building in the Worting Road, which Queen Mary's School vacated in 1940, was demolished in 1996. The Headmaster of Queen Mary's in George's time was the Rev. Chadwick, the last headmaster who was also a Clerk in Holy Orders, but it was Canon Millard who had examined George when he applied for the Aldworth Foundation Scholarship.

Sixty years after leaving school he described himself as having been 'a very shy, difficult and reserved boy'. Perhaps he felt that his remarkable intelligence set him apart from other boys. This didn't prevent him from joining in with the others in throwing snowballs on the way to school, or – in the summer months – swimming naked in the Basingstoke canal, or, as he described it, with his usual tact, when speaking to the Basingstoke Natural History Society, *in nudibus corporibus*. For a time he and other boys amused themselves by the canal making bombs, with bottles filled with gunpowder, which they managed to explode under the water. Parents put a stop to this game when one of the bombs went off when out of the water, and a friend was cut by broken glass.

Some of his happiest memories of boyhood were also of the canal, of walking back into Basingstoke on perfect summer's days. Having read *Lorna Doone* at the age of fifteen, which he had won as a school prize, he felt then that it confirmed his own feelings for the beauty of the English countryside.

In her book *Within Living Memory*, the artist and author Diana Stanley tells of two walks that were of special significance in George's life. 'About the year 1890,' she wrote,

> *George Willis and a schoolfriend were one day exploring Oliver Cromwell's Dell at Old Basing when they came upon a fragment of fossil shell in the chalk bank, and carefully extracted it. On submitting this first find to his father, young Willis was advised to take it to Mr Gilkes, the baker, at the bottom of Wote Street. When the boy entered he was led upstairs by Mr Gilkes, there to be shown a wonderful case of fossils and minerals, including a perfect specimen of the fragment he clutched in his hand.*

Having had his interest aroused, George

> *made an extensive examination of all the local chalkpits and brickfields. One day, some seven years later, when he was exploring an earthwork at Ellisfield, he happened on some flints which looked to him as though they had been rudely fashioned by hand. He took them to Dr Andrews, a local historian and archaeologist. The old doctor did not confirm his suspicion but instructed him in how to recognise flints which had been fashioned by man.'*

Later George added botany to his range of interests. He was to continue to spend nearly all his leisure time, exploring the countryside around Basingstoke searching for flints, fossils and wild flowers until old age at last overcame him.

One more strand was woven into the pattern of George's life while he was still at school. The Buckland family who lived next door, over their shop, had three sons. It was these lads who made the bombs they exploded in the canal. The youngest son Sidney was a particular friend who remembered George getting over the wall into their garden – a quicker way than going through the shop. 'We were a very scientific bunch. I fancy George was the brains of the outfit, but we all joined in the fun.' Over tea with the parents, Sidney's father William Buckland talked with enthusiasm about his interest in local politics. He was elected to the Council before the end of the century and was elected mayor in 1904. It was his example which first made George consider that serving on the Council was the best contribution he could make to his home town.

One topic must have come up in conversation at Christmas 1891, the end of George's first full year at Queen Mary's School, not only in the Buckland family but amongst all their friends. George's father had left England on a four-month visit to Sierra Leone. Together with the Rev. B. Adams, a former pastor of the Immanuel Church, he had gone to visit the mission churches there. After making his will on 4 November, he sailed from Liverpool on board the SS *Volta* on 19 December – a cold, frosty and foggy day.

How do we know what the weather was on that day, more than a hundred years ago? Our most exciting find was a letter, among the papers kept by the family, which Mr Willis wrote while on board ship, written to the Band of Hope Children, presumably members of his Sunday School. This letter reveals much of his character as well as the strongly-held views of churchgoers at that time.

After leaving the shores of Old England, when most of the passengers became ill although the sea was not rough, they reached warmer climes and anchored off Madeira on Christmas Day. When he went ashore, Mr Willis was filled with admiration for the island's beauty.

> Large trees covered with full blown camellias, palm trees, geraniums, heliotropes and a great many others were growing and blooming in the open and the sun was shining so bright and warm it seemed like a heavenly place to me.

There was, however, a shadow over Paradise.

> But though everything around is so beautiful – beautiful hills and flowers, trees and sunshine – yet there is much here to make one sad. The bulk of the people are Roman Catholics and they think that if they go to Mass that is all they need do. They hear no sermons and their children have no nice meetings as you have – their only teachers are the priests who in many cases are quite ignorant of salvation through Jesus Christ. Oh children you ought to be so thankful that God has sent kind teachers who will teach you right things and help you to be good.

The letter ends with the hope that the children are 'being obedient to your teachers and above all to your loving Saviour', and is signed 'Your affectionate friend, G.W. Willis'. The article in *The Harbinger*, where we first learned of this trip to Africa, said that Mr Willis took a large number of photographs which have been mounted as lantern slides and are available to any for the purpose of exhibition. Now if they are still about, that would be a find!

How the firm of G.W. Willis survived the absence of the owner on this four-month trip to Africa is hard to understand. Emily Perkins was only twenty-six and presumably only sold watches and jewellery over the counter. Possibly other watchmakers in the town helped. There was not the same feeling then that you were only successful when you had put your competitors out of business. The firm did survive and three years later, in 1894, when young George left Queen Mary's School he joined his father, learning the trade at the bench at the back of the shop where he was to go on working, almost until he died. Whether George knew then that this was the work he wanted to do, or whether it was a case of obedience to his father, we shall never know. We do know that from then on, for the rest of his life, that work bench provided him with the most permanent, stable element in his life. His terms of office as Church treasurer, councillor, magistrate, curator of the museum he created, came to an end. His house was destroyed in World War 2. That work bench was always there.

Working together, the father and son were building up the business. No job was too small or too large. A bill-head, dated June 1896, showed they charged Mrs Bacon 3 pence (about 1p) for repairing a pepper box, and some years later £2/10/– (£2.50) for winding and attending clocks at Hackwood House for one year. In the earlier years of the firm farm workers would come in for a watch which was to last them a lifetime – the larger the better. At a much earlier period a farm worker in the Basingstoke area who kept a diary, and whose wife, after bearing him eleven children, lived to be 94, wrote, '1856 was notable from the fact that on July 9th baught a watch from Mr William Grigory (B'toke) £1-15 which I paid'.

Watchmakers and Jewellers at that time were also opticians, and continued to practise as such well into the next century. As well as being opticians the firm of G.W. Willis was also advertising, in 1899, that

> *Mr T. Godfrey, Surgeon, Dentist of Regent Street, London attends at Mr Willis, watchmakers and jeweller, every Wednesday from 10.30 a.m. to 4 p.m. – noted for his patent artificial teeth and for gold fillings.*

As the century drew to a close and Queen Victoria's Diamond Jubilee had been celebrated, with more processions, more cheers and singing of the National Anthem, and meals for the poor at tables set out in the Market Place, so the first signs appeared of the changes that were to take place. George had been given a bicycle while still at school and recalled an occasion when, after a detachment of the Royal Artillery had spent the night in Basingstoke while on their way to the West Country for manoeuvres, with the guns parked in the Market Place overnight, he had followed the gun carriages to Overton. Then the first motor cars were seen and, in 1898, Mr Watson, who had a business repairing bicycles, became the first person in Basingstoke to own a motor car. This was a Coventry two-seater which, as George noted and remembered, had open flame ignition instead of sparking plugs and a twelve-inch (30 cm) diameter gear wheel. These early cars were extremely noisy. Whenever Mr Watson's car was heard people rushed in his direction to see it. The Government had fixed the speed limit for motor vehicles at 12 m.p.h. in 1896 so it wasn't too difficult to catch a sight of Mr Watson's car. At least that was the case in the town. He probably went rather faster in the countryside.

So the nineteenth century came to an end, with Queen Victoria still on the throne, and there seemed no doubt that the firm of G.W. Willis would grow and enjoy the years of prosperity that lay ahead. Then in May 1900 George's father suffered a stroke. He recovered enough to be able to get about but his working days were over. At the early age of twenty-two George found himself running the business.

Chapter Two
1900–1916 Head of the Family

'Nothing to do and nowhere to go'

A photograph, in the family collection, taken by a professional photographer in Bristol, shows a well-built man, wearing a large beard of the type popular at the end of the last century. The face of this man, who has avoided looking at the camera, has the fixed look to be seen in the faces of people who have suffered a stroke. Behind the man are a young woman and two young girls. It is reasonably certain that this shows the elder George Willis with his three daughters, Ellen Mary now nearly twenty, Edith Bessie who was born in 1889, and Dorothy Elsie, the youngest of the family, who was not born until 1894. They are on a visit to the Acklands – their relatives in Bristol. Mrs Willis and their son are presumably left in Basingstoke, looking after the shop.

Although he had been unable to return to his work as watchmaker and jeweller, the elder George Willis was able to get about and enjoy the company of friends and relatives. On Monday evening, 3 November 1902, he was saying goodbye to friends at Basingstoke's railway station when he suffered another stroke. His son was with him. Dr Miller was called and soon arrived. Mr Willis was placed in a cab. The horse galloped down Station Hill and up Wote Street but before the cab reached the shop, Mr Willis had died.

At the funeral, the pastor of the Immanuel Church spoke at the graveside of the 'deceased's Christian work and especially his interest and affection for the little ones'. The family, who were wearing the mourning clothes bought with the £30 thoughtfully provided by Mr Willis in his will, were joined by a considerable number of the members of the Wote Street congregation. As well as the wreaths they gave, there was a floral spray from Sir Wyndham and Lady Portal.

Years later, speaking of 'his difficult adolescence', George Willis remembered 'one occasion when he had felt in the town in which he was born that he had nothing to do and nowhere to go'. Now the path his life was to follow had been decided for him. Quite apart from his father's will which left the estate to his mother during her lifetime, then to be shared among himself and his three sisters, he had the moral responsibility of supporting them. John Arlott took the view that George's commitment to his native town was a conscious decision. I am not so sure. In different circumstances he might have led a different life.

His father had made that historic journey to Africa. His youngest sister was to spend many years in Africa. All three of the Buckland boys, who were neighbours, settled abroad, the elder two in Africa and his friend Sid in Canada. I am quite sure, though, that George accepted the responsibility put upon him with the same equanimity with which he treated all the successes and failures of his long life.

George also took on some of the offices his father had held in the Immanuel Church. The year after his father's death he was appointed treasurer, a post he was to hold for the next twenty years. He was also a member of the Church Committee, possibly for a longer time. One letter from an old friend shows that he assisted with the Sunday School but this may have been at an earlier period. 'My memory goes back to Sunday school days when even then you were trying to help troublesome lads, such as I was, to pass a certain time of leisure time to some advantage – hand bell ringing etc.'

The firm was renamed 'G.W. Willis & Son'. The 'son' became Mr Willis and was to be known by that name for the rest of his life. This was, of course, the custom of his times. I remember, in the early 60s, the vicar of Basingstoke causing much concern among the older members of the congregation by suggesting that after the service we should greet each other, using our Christian names. But he was still George, I am sure, to the young men who had been his school companions.

It appears that this was the time when Mr Willis ceased exploring the countryside around Basingstoke for fossils, flints and wild flowers. It was the beginning of the ten-year gap in the pursuit of his hobbies to which he referred in later years. Probably he simply couldn't spare the time for these long walks.

To a casual observer Basingstoke had not changed very much as the Victorian age had been replaced by the Edwardian period. More people were riding bicycles, and a few more people owned cars, and also motor bikes. By July 1904 the number of vehicles registered in the county of Hampshire was 351 cars and 401 motorcycles; 1093 persons were licensed to drive. Horses still provided the main means of transport, except when it was more convenient to go by train. Goods which came to the town by train were delivered by horse-drawn van. Country people coming into town came in horse-drawn wagons.

One particular occasion that Mr Willis remembered was the night which a brigade of the City Imperial Volunteers spent in Basingstoke during the Boer War. They were a mounted brigade and their horses were drawn up in the Market Place. With his usual aptitude for observing and remembering details, George was struck by the rawness and newness of their leather equipment, so different to the well-worn, dark brown equipment of the men of the Artillery who had stopped in Basingstoke in earlier years.

A few months before his father died, Basingstoke had celebrated the coronation of His Majesty King Edward VII. Carriages, with their horses no doubt specially groomed for the occasion, waited in Wote Street before joining the procession which began and ended in the Market Place, stopping at intervals, as it went round the town, so that everyone could give 'three cheers for the King'. In the evening there was a concert in the Market Place, given by the Viennese Band.

Horses were used for several more years for pulling the two fire engines which were kept under the floor at the north end of the Corn Exchange, where the road was much lower than the floor. The landlord of *The Barge* was responsible for providing the horses, four to each engine, when the alarm was raised by ringing a bell mounted on the roof of the Corn Exchange. The horses were always made to gallop up Wote Street as they started off.

The most memorable fire in this period was the one which demolished Burberry's shop in Winchester Street in 1905. An assistant had been decorating a shop window for Christmas when cotton wool being used for the decorations caught fire – possibly caused by an overturned lamp. By the time the fire had been brought under control so much damage had been caused that this, the largest shop in town, had to be entirely rebuilt. Mr Willis remembered how they all rushed out of the shop on hearing the bell being rung.

Christmas seems to have been a bad time for fires. An earlier occasion was the fire in 1901 which severely damaged the Buckland's shop next door to them.

> It happened in the winter, just before Christmas, on a very frosty night. The water froze on the ladders and all down the street the ground was like glass. One of the girls in the building had a narrow escape, as the front bedrooms were all burnt out. She had her "bottom drawer" full of things in preparation for her wedding, but bedsteads and drawers all fell into the flames.

Perhaps Mr Willis, with his mother and sisters, was encouraged by this fire to stop living over the shop. After his father's death, they moved to a house in Cliddesden Road, on the south side of the town. It was much quieter here, no longer with the door of the shop opening on to the street, and further away from the sounds of the Town Hall clock chiming every quarter of an hour and goods trains being shunted at the station all through the night. The house also had a large garden where some of the best family photos were taken – Mr Willis, wearing a high collar, slim, neat, with his mother in front of him and his three very good-looking sisters, in long dresses, beside him.

Although he left the shop in the evening to go home, leaving a tenant upstairs acting as a caretaker, George was still very much a member of the community of tradespeople who were in charge of the town's affairs. *Kelly's Directory* of 1899 shows the domination they had in this period. All the sixteen aldermen and councillors were 'in trade'. Colonel John May, the brewer, who had been mayor four times, was an alderman. Mr Gerrish, clothing manufacturer, was a councillor. There was a horse dealer, a hay and straw salesman, an engineer, and the rest were ironmongers, builders, grocers, butchers and Mr Willis's neighbour Mr Buckland who sold a wide range of fancy goods. The names of all these men appear on the list of burgesses which was drawn up and published each year by the 'Churchwardens and Overseers of the Poor'. The burgesses had the right to vote for councillors, based on ownership of property.

Although he was much younger than the owners of most other firms in the town, it seems reasonable to assume that Mr Willis was popular and well known. His father had laid the foundations for a successful business, with both a growing trade among local people, and good contacts with landowners in the country around Basingstoke, whose clocks the firm serviced. The floral spray which Sir Wyndham and Lady Portal had sent to the senior Mr Willis's funeral gives some idea of the respect in which his father was held. In 1954, when the son was made Freeman of Basingstoke, Sir Charles Chute recalled

> *the first time [he] saw Mr Willis when, as a very young man then learning the business, he accompanied a clock-maker from Basingstoke to assist in the upkeep of the clocks of his grandfather's house at Malshanger. That was in the last century and that showed that even at that time the presence of Mr Willis impressed itself at all events on someone.*

The events that gave excitement or colour to the life of this quiet market town were recorded week by week in the *Hants & Berks Gazette*. The appearance of Basingstoke was recorded on the postcards published in this period and held in private collections. The type of information

Mr Willis sought, on archaeology, history and botany was not so easily obtained. The sources of information we can use today, some of which had not been envisaged at the turn of the century, were not available in Basingstoke.

There were small lending libraries to be found in many shops but I doubt whether they kept the sort of reference books Mr Willis would have wanted to consult. The best library, with over 2000 volumes, was the one to be found in the Mechanics' Institute and Club. This was affiliated to the London Working Men's Club and Union. It was established in 1841 and moved into a building, designed for its particular use and built in New Street, which was opened by the Rev. Charles Kingsley – best known as the author of *The Water Babies* – on 13 October 1869. By a curious coincidence Mr Willis had been born exactly eight years later. The library had a membership of around 300 which remained fairly constant. From the beginning the lectures that were given there would have been difficult for many working men to follow. The topics on which lectures were given in the year the Institute was founded included 'Mental culture as a means of combating social backwardness and political despotism', 'The Mechanical Properties of Steam' and 'Ornithology'. Many of the local gentry were patrons and probably attended meetings.

More than anywhere else in Basingstoke it was the place where Mr Willis, still thirsting for knowledge, would feel at home. We have found no record of the date when he joined. Possibly George Gage, who had been his headmaster at both the British School and the Board School, may have introduced him. Mr Willis could have had no idea, when he first walked into the Mechanics' Institute, of the part that organisation and that building would play in his life.

One of the happiest occasions of this period was his sister Ellen's wedding on 11 March 1909, described in great detail by the *Hants & Berks Gazette*.

The Immanuel Church was crowded with eager sightseers on Thursday afternoon on the occasion of the marriage of Mr Bernard Charles Jukes and Miss Ellen Mary Willis, both of whom deservedly enjoy the respect of a wide circle of friends in the town.

The service was conducted by the bridegroom's father, who had been a missionary in Madagascar. He was assisted by the pastor of the Congregational Church – the Jukes were Congregationalists – and the pastor of the Immanuel Church.

The rich tones of Wagner's Bridal Chorus pealed forth from the organ as the bride, escorted by her uncle, Mr F.J. Ackland, proceeded up the aisle ... The bride looked charming in her dress of ivory collientie, made in the Directoire style ... Lilies formed the principal feature of the bridal bouquet she was carrying.

At the end of the report, the paper listed the wedding presents and the donors. Mr George Willis gave a Brazilian onyx clock.

After the reception held at the Lecture Hall in May Place – attached to the Congregational Church – the couple left for Bournemouth on the 4.37 train. The only item of interest which the paper didn't include was how they got to the station. In the adjoining column Mr Watson was advertising 'Good Cars for Hire'. Could it have been his 30 h.p. Humber, with or without a cover, and with a reliable driver?

Bernard Jukes was a chemist. His shop was next door to the Immanuel Church. At the time of writing it still has the name of Jukes over the shop front but the building is empty. The shop has spacious accommodation on two floors over it and this was to be home for Mr and Mrs Jukes and their two children for many years.

Mr Willis first entered public service in 1913 when, on 6 March, he was appointed by the Basingstoke Town Council as an 'Overseer of the Poor'. The overseers were not councillors, nor were they elected by the people. Each year the outgoing overseers drew up a list of men they considered suitable for the post, and the choice of names was made by the Council. In 1913 the name of Mr Willis was one of eight chosen from a list of twenty-four. He remained an overseer until the post was abolished by the Rating and Valuation Act of 1925 on 1 April 1927. At first the responsibility he was being given alarmed him.

Aware, he said, of his extreme ignorance of such matters and expecting to have to make far-reaching decisions, he was filled with consternation until, at the first meeting, he found old school pals around the table who were no more expert than himself. The transactions of the overseers, handwritten in two minute books covering a period of thirty-six years, give the impression that the task was not too onerous. They were responsible for collecting the Poor Rate and for deciding who should be excused from paying this, on the grounds of their own poverty, but the actual collection was done by the an official called the 'Assistant Overseer'.

This year – 1913 – was also the year when, in conversation at the Mechanics' Institute with John Ellaway, who was a fellow member of the committee, George mentioned his old hobby of collecting flints, and aroused John's interest. The two men agreed to go for a walk together at Wellocks Hill, a site already known to George Willis as one where he had found fragments of Roman pottery. John Ellaway quickly developed an aptitude and liking for the hobby.

John Ellaway worked in the offices of Wallis and Steevens, the iron founders and builders of agricultural machinery and road rollers. Like George he was self-educated after leaving school. He delighted in books, enjoyed literary competitions, was an avid reader of booksellers' catalogues, had a retentive memory and was the obvious person to become Basingstoke's first librarian. He was an ideal companion for Mr Willis, whose own capacity for reading and absorbing knowledge was exceptional. After John Ellaway died, George Willis wrote,

His name will always bring back to me memories – of sun-scorched ploughed fields, of wind-swept frozen hillsides, of quiet rides in flowery woods, of ancient tracks and burial mounds on open downs, of little churches in remote valleys, of nightingales singing in sunny copses, of pockets full of dusty flints and Roman pottery, and of thirty years of unbroken comradeship.

Two years after he and John Ellaway started exploring the countryside together, Mr Willis became a member of the Hampshire Field Club. As well as having the *Proceedings* of the Club to read, membership brought him into contact with the leading archaeologists, historians and botanists of the Hampshire area.

Collecting fossils, flints and other archaeological remains was never an end in itself. Finding these artefacts was the way to discover how our ancient ancestors had lived. An article, by G.W. Willis, called 'Flinting round Basingstoke', was published by the *Hants & Berks Gazette*, in parts, over a three-week period in 1914. Mr Willis used much of the first part to describe how suitable the Basingstoke district was as a home for Neolithic man. Water – the primary necessity for life – came out of chalk springs. The high ground to the south of the present town afforded good visibility. The marshes which then existed in the valleys also provided security for these hill-dwellers. There was an abundance of trees for making homes, food – fish, flesh and fowl – in the marshes, and flints for making tools could be found where the hills were covered with a layer of clay containing them.

It was in the same period that Mr Willis was watching the excavation involved with the building of the new road, to be named Penrith Road, at the bottom of Sarum Hill. Where the road cut through a bank of earth, burnt soil containing blackened stones on a base of gravel was revealed. Mr Willis realised that in prehistoric time this had been a cooking area beside a stream, the stones, known as 'pot-boilers', being heated in the fire and dropped into vessels to heat the water in them. Mr Willis was thrilled to think that he was one of the first people for centuries to see this site where our early ancestors had squatted beside the stream, waiting for the water in their clay vessels to warm up. Others could travel the world. He could travel in time, discovering the way people had lived in the past.

Both he and John Ellaway wanted to share these discoveries with their fellow citizens. They believed that the artefacts they were collecting should be displayed where others could see them. The idea of a museum for Basingstoke was beginning to take shape.

It is unfortunate that the reputation Mr Willis has as an antiquarian often obscures the fact that he was as curious and clear-sighted about the future as he was about the past. The years between his leaving school and World War 1 starting covered the period during which inventions in mechanisation, transport and communication – then being developed by engineers and scientists in Europe and America – would change the way in which the world's industrial nations lived. England's rural way of life would disappear. Basingstoke would need to find a new role, apart from serving this rural economy.

Whenever these new inventions were first seen in Basingstoke Mr Willis was present. He remembered visiting his namesake Ted Willis, who was no relation, to hear what was probably the first wireless set in the town, and how thrilled he was to realise he was hearing someone speaking from London. On another occasion X-rays were demonstrated during a lecture in the Town Hall. The first showing of a cinema film was in the Corn Exchange.

> *When the show opened we saw a rather dingy yellowish still of vehicles and pedestrians on a London bridge. Then suddenly they all started to move, and I well recall the 'Oh' that went up from the crowded audience. The picture flickered terribly and the film was old and scratched, but to unsophisticated Basingstoke it was wonderful.*

Mr Willis was not content just to see this new way of life emerging. He wanted to be part of it. Some time before World War 1, he bought a motor bike. This was a Swiss-made Moto-Reeve. It looks like a motorised bicycle but can travel some 100 miles on a tank full of petrol and has a maximum speed of 30–35 m.p.h. His motor bike is one of the exhibits which will be seen in Basingstoke's new Transport Museum, being built at the time of writing.

In the early part of 1914 Mr Willis was pre-occupied with the present rather than the past or the future. After being ill for three months with heart problems, his mother died at home on Tuesday evening, 7 April. The *Hants & Berks Gazette* remembered her as an ardent temperance worker associated for many years with the British Women's Temperance Association. Her son followed her example in being prepared to campaign for causes he believed in, although they were different causes. Mr Willis was not a teetotaller, but was only a modest drinker, content with a glass of cider when attending Rotary Club meetings or the annual Old Boys' Association dinner. His sister Nellie was influenced – not only by her mother but by seeing a drunken child lying in the gutter – to become as active as her mother in supporting the temperance movement.

By the end of the year Britain was at war – the Great War that was to end all wars, as everyone believed at the time. It was some consolation to Mr Willis and his sisters that their mother had not lived long enough to see this. Mr Willis was nearly 37, too old then to feel he should volunteer and see his name appear in the Roll of Honour which was published regularly in the local paper, listing the volunteers. There was still the shop to manage and his sisters to support. They continued to live in Cliddesden Road.

Mr Willis did, however, believe he could play a part in the life of the town, if he was elected a councillor. According to his own account, to Councillor Tigwell's and to John Arlott's, Mr Willis stood for election in 1914 and lost by about 50 votes, but I have found no confirmation that he ever stood for election in 1914. There was an election, reported in the *Hants & Berks Gazette*, in November 1914. The name of Mr Willis does not appear in the list of candidates. We could find no references to other elections in that year, nor did his name appear in 1913. The minute books and other records of the Borough Council are now kept in the Public Record Office but neither we nor the archivists could find any reference to Mr Willis there.

After 1914 no more elections were held in wartime, and then in August 1916 the name of George Willis was proposed by Councillor W.H. Tigwell to fill the vacancy caused by the resignation of Councillor Sollom. He reminded his fellow councillors that Mr Willis had once stood for election, and that he was a man they all knew. Councillor Powell drew attention to the fact that Mr Willis was of military age. Councillor Tigwell replied that he had been refused. No other person was proposed and the co-option of Mr Willis was unanimously agreed.

A 1885 *Ellen, George senior, Sarah, George (8)*

B 1887 *Town Hall decorated for Queen Victoria's Golden Jubilee*

C 1897 *Family group in the garden behind the shop in Wote Street –
George (20), Sarah, Dorothy, Edith, George senior, Ellen*

D 1901 *Photo taken at Weston-super-Mare – George senior, Edith, Dorothy,
Ellen*

E 1912 *Family group in the garden at Cliddesden Road – Edith, Sarah, George (35), Brian Jukes (2), Bernard Jukes, Ellen, Dorothy*

F 1915 *George (38), Ted Willis (no relation) and Percy Grover*

Chapter Three
1916–1926 Mayor of Basingstoke

'... the peace which comes when one finds one's niche in life ...'

The reaction of Mr Willis, now that he had achieved the position he had tried for two years earlier, was to panic. He did not think there was ever a more raw, shy and difficult recruit to the Council than himself. He remembered kicking himself in the afternoon for not having the moral courage to stand up and say the things he ought to have done at the Council meeting in the morning. The Council was going through a difficult time. The handling of the town's finances was being scrutinised week by week in the *Hants & Berks Gazette*, in both reports and correspondence.

The mayor was Thomas Allnutt, who had been first elected to the Council in 1892, and elected Mayor in 1915, a position he was to hold until 1919. He was then a retired businessman. He belonged to the London Street Congregational Church and was a staunch adherent to the Liberal Party. The war imposed additional heavy duties on the mayor. He was chairman of the Borough Tribunal which sat 80 times during the war. The Food Control Committee and the War Savings Committee were two of the committees he chaired. He raised money for the Red Cross and other war-time causes. Years later he played a key role in furthering Mr Willis's ambition, but neither man could have foreseen this in 1916.

In some ways the people of Basingstoke were suffering terribly after two years of war, as fathers, mothers, wives, sisters and younger brothers dreaded the postman calling, fearing he would bring one of the black-edged envelopes with news that a loved one had died on the battle field. It was difficult to forget the fighting with so many soldiers about the town. You saw them marching from the station to the vast camp which had been set up on the common. When you saw them on their way back to the station you knew they were on their way to Southampton to embark for France. Some families had soldiers billeted on them. The firm of Thorneycroft had grown into a major manufacturer of military vehicles.

Yet in other ways life went on much as it had done in peacetime. Munday's *Basingstoke Directory*, published in 1916, carried an advertisement showing that Webbers Motor Garage had 'New cars in stock for immediate delivery'. Butchers could supply the best English meat. Grocers offered 'the best Cheddar, Stiltons, Gorgonzolas etc. to be obtained anywhere'. New milk was delivered twice daily to any part of the town. Several shops were making wedding cakes to order. Clothes rationing had not been thought of, and one builder would fit special dancing floors to suit the size of your rooms!

G.W. Willis & Son, Watchmakers, Jewellers, Ophthalmic Opticians were offering a large selection of silver, plate, clocks etc. as suitable wedding presents. It is perhaps surprising to find from the advertisements Mr Willis inserted, week after week, in the *Hants & Berks Gazette* that he had a remarkable flair for advertising the business which his self-effacing personality would never have suggested. Unlike most other Basingstoke firms, he frequently changed the layout of his advertisements. One of the cleverest was used when the 'Daylight Saving Act' of 1916 came into force. Mr Willis set out, in bold letters, 'Hints to Householders on "putting on the clock".' There was no need to wait until two in the morning before changing the time, and 'If in spite of your care a clock subsequently refuses to show "Summer Time" accurately, don't try drastic remedies of your own, but submit it to the experts – G.W. Willis & Son.'

The war did not, apparently, stop him and John Ellaway from searching the countryside around Basingstoke for the flints and other artefacts left by our distant ancestors. The *Proceedings* of the Hampshire Field Club for 1916 includes a report by Dr Williams-Freeman of information supplied by Mr Willis. Considerable additions had been made to the collections of local flint implements. The Kempshott area had been found to be an unusually rich source. Three workers in the field, for some years, had been collecting, on average, an annual total of 450 specimens. The reference to three workers shows that Mr Willis and Mr Ellaway had already been joined by Mr Rainbow.

As well as finding flint implements, these three men had identified some twenty tumuli sites, which were not shown on the 6-inch ordnance survey maps and which were duly placed on the Field Club maps. These sites are all within a few miles of Basingstoke.

From 1920 Mr Willis was the local reporter to the Hampshire Field Club. When the Club celebrated its centenary in 1985, an article in the *Proceedings* named Mr Willis as one of four men who were most active in the period 1905 to 1920. The other three were Dr Williams-Freeman, Mr Sumner and Mr Crawford. Considering that Mr Willis only appeared on the scene in the last years of that period it is remarkable that he should have made such an impact in such a short time.

A report that Mr Willis made for the *Proceedings* of the Club in 1928 shows the scientific approach he brought to his studies. During the year

706 flint implements had been found by him and his colleagues. These were divided into six groups, the largest of which were scrapers, of which they found 369. There were also 152 flints in a miscellaneous section. The total number of flints found was a little lower than the yearly average, but the general percentage of the various types of instruments found remained extraordinarily constant. It is possible that Mr Rainbow – the 'meticulous' Mr Rainbow – helped in sorting the flints out and analysing the numbers.

When the war did come to an end it was not until the next July that Basingstoke held formal peace celebrations. They started with a parade of returned service men at 11.30 a.m. They were later given a dinner. In the afternoon there were children's sports, and in the evening there were bands giving concerts, followed by dancing until one in the morning. Mr Willis was a member of the committee which organised the event.

Probably the most noticeable change to be seen in Basingstoke when the war ended was the disappearance of soldiers from the streets. After the camp on the common was dismantled, Mr Willis took the opportunity carefully to inspect the ground where mules had been kept. At first it looked as if the pasture had been ruined. During long spells of wet weather the ground had been trodden into a quagmire. Yet the next season there was a phenomenal growth of grass up to 3 or 4 feet (1–3 m) in height. The plants which Mr Willis found amongst this grass are described in the last paragraph of an article he wrote for the *Hants & Berks Gazette* on 'Basingstoke Common and the Enclosure Award'.

And as the mules had been fed on imported fodder there grew among the grass a strange variety of alien plants that were a continual surprise and delight to the exploring botanist – plants often far removed from anything in the British flora. Most of these strangers were traced to North America, whence the fodder had been brought. By the next season all this exotic growth had entirely disappeared and the Common resumed its normal appearance and now, apart from a small persistent patch of Meadow Saxifrage in the middle, a curious development of Crow Garlic along the northern border, and the tiny white flowers of the Mud Crowfoot on the muddy banks of its water, the Common holds only the wild flowers of the English field and hedgerow.

This passage provides a perfect illustration of Mr Willis's ability to observe accurately, draw conclusions from his observations and retain this knowledge in his memory for very long periods of time. The article, of which this paragraph forms only five per cent, was published over twenty years later, in 1941. The rest of the article recounts the history of the common through the centuries, much of which is taken from old documents which were then kept by the Council. He may have recounted his natural history observations in some other publication. If he kept notebooks we have found no trace of them. They are not held at the museum in Basingstoke or at the County headquarters near Winchester where we would have expected to find them. In this respect he differed from Gilbert White, who kept a daily journal. In other ways the two men had much in common. Gilbert White, born a hundred and fifty years earlier, was also educated at Basingstoke and then spent his life studying the natural history of Selborne in the same way that George Willis studied the history and flora of the Basingstoke area.

The death in 1920 of Colonel John May, who had been mayor five times, removed from the Basingstoke scene the most flamboyant character of the last century. He was buried in the cemetery near the railway station, where John Arlott's father was the cemetery keeper. The principal mourners following the coffin wore top hats. It may have been the last occasion of this style. At the time evidence of the Colonel's munificence could be seen in every part of the town. The clock tower on the Town Hall and the lamp standard in Market Place, the drill hall, an extension to the cottage hospital and the cricket ground, known as May's Bounty, were all examples of his philanthropy. Today all that remains is the cricket ground where Hampshire play for one week of the summer.

The year after the Colonel's death the Town Council took on his role by purchasing 'Goldings', a large house on the London road, on the east side of the town, together with the grounds, comprising 23 acres. The house was used for council offices and the grounds became the Memorial Park with a memorial to the fallen being erected just inside the gates. The bandstand was brought from the Fairfields Recreation Ground. Mr Allnutt, who had been mayor during the war years, actively promoted this project and Thomas Burberry made the purchase possible by lending the money to the Council. This was certainly an improvement to the town which Mr Willis must have strongly supported.

In one of his articles on Mr Willis, John Arlott tells of him going away to Hook, five miles up the London road, to convalesce after having had his appendix removed in 1914. He was certainly travelling further afield in the years after the war. He spent a holiday at Westward Ho in 1924. This was, most likely, one of the times when he travelled with Tom

Pettle, the manager of Bowman's drapery stores in Market Place. Tom came from Braunton, in north Devon, the other side of the River Taw from Westward Ho, and went home to visit his fiancée. The two men rode on their motor bikes, taking two days for the journey and camping overnight on Salisbury Plain. Tom's bike was similar to George's Moto-Reeve. They often had to stop to mend punctures. George's holidays were an opportunity to indulge in his favourite recreation – walking. He often went away with friends, and is remembered as going away for a week every May.

At a meeting of the Immanuel Church Committee, held in January 1923, Mr Willis stated that he wished to resign from the position of treasurer, a position he had held for twenty years, owing to pressure of other public business. Did Mr Willis have some intuition that before the year ended he would be Basingstoke's mayor? He wasn't due to serve in that office until the following year. Did he continue to worship at the Immanuel Church or anywhere else? None of the people living today remembers him attending any place of worship except for weddings, funerals or civic occasions. Sunday was a day set aside for walking in the countryside. Walking was a lifelong passion. It was probably an essential way to relax from the pressure of work and civic responsibility. Apart from occasional attacks of lumbago he enjoyed good health which must have been helped by this regular exercise. Dr Potter told me, 'I was his doctor for over forty years but his natural stamina was no less remarkable than his moral fibre and intellectual resources.'

In October 1923 Mr Willis was elected as an alderman to fill the vacancy caused by the resignation of Alderman John Knowles who had retired to Torquay. About the same time Mr Willis agreed to stand for mayor, the election falling due the next month.

Councillors have sometimes told me that they hoped they would have the opportunity to serve as mayor before they retired from the Council. I am sure such a thought never entered Mr Willis's mind. For him it was a daunting challenge which he had a moral duty to accept.

The *Hants & Berks Gazette* reported the proceedings of the election of the mayor in full under the simple heading 'Basingstoke Town Council: Election of Mayor'. It was almost a verbatim report. During the Great War there had been at least one page each week reporting the progress of the war. Earlier still the paper covered national and international events as well as reporting on happenings in the Hampshire and Berkshire region, with often only a few columns on Basingstoke. Perhaps our town was now being recognised as a place of some importance.

The meeting of the Council was held at noon, leaving time for the luncheon which was to follow. The election of Mr Willis was proposed by Alderman Hillary who said that when Mr Willis had been approached he had replied,

I was not looking for it yet, but it is my duty to take it, and whatever my personal feelings may be, as a matter of duty I am prepared to take it.' Seconding the nomination Mr G.T. Pheby said that he had served on several committees with Mr Willis and had always found him a level-headed man, and one who had helped them to get out of a tight corner. In Mr Willis they had a man who would watch the interests of the town in general.

Having been elected, invested with the Mayoral robe and chain, signed the declaration of office and taken the necessary oaths, the new Mayor thanked the Council for the great honour they had done him. He had been encouraged by the friendly greetings he had received to hope that he might, without entire failure at any rate, carry through the duties of this office. It was a peculiar pleasure for him that Mr Buckland, now once more a Councillor, whose pupil in municipal affairs he had been as a young man, was one of those who had elected him.

Mr Willis said that he was only too conscious of his own drawbacks. There was one obvious drawback that he had preached to him repeatedly. Unlike his predecessors, there was no official Mayoress in the ordinary sense of the word. Happily Providence had helped him with sisters, and he was glad to say that one of them (his eldest sister Nellie Jukes) was willing to occupy this position, thus enabling him to escape that very desperate remedy that had been repeatedly urged upon him. (Laughter)

Another more genuine difficulty was that his predecessors in office were employers on a big scale and had been accustomed to handling business on a bigger scale than he had been used to. He was afraid that he would require more help from the officers of the council than others had done. Having dealt with his drawbacks Mr Willis went on to describe his view of the duties of his office. It was to be more than a reconciliation of conflicting interests. He believed that it should be a proud thing for a man to be a citizen of Basingstoke, 'a citizen of no mean city'. He was interested in the forward look – what Basingstoke might become.

Before he sat down he spoke of town planning, and the promotion of a Bill for the proper control of the local resources of the town. The new Mayor had made it clear he would try to steer the town in the direction he believed it should go.

After the official business had been completed, the councillors were joined by invited guests for the Mayor's Luncheon. Mr Willis had sent out the invitations before his election, the correspondence having been carried out by an exchange of letters, all handwritten. During the luncheon the guests were entertained by music provided by a small orchestra, the arrangement having been in the capable hands of Mr A.G. Wood who was the organist at the Immanuel Church.

After the loyal toasts had been drunk, followed by a toast to the retiring Mayor, the health of the new Mayor was proposed by Mr T.B. Allnutt, who had been Mayor during the war years when Mr Willis first joined the Council. He noted that Mr Willis was a native of Basingstoke, born, bred and educated here. Such circumstances must add to the feeling of local patriotism which everyone ought to have. During the seven years Mr Willis had been on the Council, they had all been impressed by his capable handling of affairs and in particular for his work as Chairman of the Water Supply Committee. Mr Allnutt then returned to the problem of the Mayor's bachelor status. Mr Willis laboured under one disadvantage – he was not blessed with a good wife to share his anxieties and pleasures. (Laughter) This was a misfortune which could be cured and ought not to be endured. (Laughter) When the Town Clerk spoke he drew attention to one point which had been missed, and that was that next year was Leap Year. (Laughter) He thought it was up to the ladies of Basingstoke on the 29th February next year to do their best; and he wished success to the best of them (Renewed laughter).

Sir Arthur Holbrook, MP, who proposed the toast of of the town and trade of Basingstoke took a more serious line, concentrating, as politicians often do on these occasions, on the economic problems facing the country and the need to restrict the import of foreign goods. He noted that Basingstoke was placed in a very favourable position as regards railway communication and he hoped full advantage would be taken of these facilities by the establishment of new factories. The three business men who responded to the MP were Tom Thornycroft, now probably the largest employer in the town, the Mayor's brother-in-law Bernard Jukes and Mr Gerrish who manufactured the clothing sold by Mr Burberry.

Among the letters of congratulation which Mr Willis received there were two which caught my attention. The Secretary of the Trustees of the Countess of Hungtingdon's Connexion, writing from London, wrote,

> I pray that you may have health, wisdom and heavenly guidance to worthily fulfil all the duties of the office in such a way as to serve God and honour the King.'

Margaret Hardy, writing from the Midlands, took a different line.

> Dear Mr Mayor
> I must send you congratulations.
> But what a life. Bazaars and Salvation Army tea-fights for a man of science! At least you will have to practise 'Coueism' [systematic auto-suggestion, from Emile Coue, a French psychologist] to a certain extent, and make suggestions to the churches and such places (or bodies) in which you don't greatly believe. Perhaps by the end of the time you will have suggested yourself into a condition of belief, or affection for them at all events.
> I wonder if you will enjoy it all.
> Best of wishes, Margaret Hardy
> PS My kindest regards to the Mayoress

Margaret's teasing letter suggests that she was someone on the same intellectual level as Mr Willis. She went on to talk of taking up an appointment with a Congregational Church so she may have met Mr Willis at the London Street Church in Basingstoke, or else, possibly at the Mechanics' Institute. John Shields, who did not meet Mr Willis until after World War 2, described him as 'a liberal and free thinker, who was always tolerant of other people's religious views'.

Other letters, kept at the Hampshire Record Office, give a random sample of the mayor's activities. The Basingstoke Victory Choir, which was to be renamed the Basingstoke Choral Society, asked him to be vice-president. The Wesleyan Sunday School asked him to support their anniversary meeting. Would the mayor preside at the annual meeting of the Hants County Nursing Association?

There are letters from the MP replying to the mayor's request for help in improving the rail service to London. Lieut-Cdr R. Fletcher, RN, a member of the Liberal Party, was now Member of Parliament, having taken the seat from the Conservative Sir Arthur Holbrook. Letters about the rail service and other letters suggest the two men had soon become good friends.

At a local level Mr Willis took a particular interest in the War Memorial Park, ensuring that it should be equipped to provide good facilities for recreation for all. He arranged that music should be provided every week, under the direction of his friend Mr Wood, who freely gave his time for this activity. There were also some special occasions when the mayor represented the town. One was the enthronement of the new Bishop of Winchester and another was the opening of the new floating dock at Southampton, in June 1924, when he had lunch, on board the *Aquitania* with HRH the Prince of Wales. He attended the opening of the great Wembley Exhibition of 1924.

When I was president of the Basingstoke District Chamber of Commerce for a year I found I had little time, apart from my work, for other activities. The mayor and I often met at the same functions, but I was always aware that for every meeting I had to chair, every function I had to attend, the mayor probably had ten. In 1923 the Mayor may have had fewer demands on his time, but on the other hand the mayor was also the Chief Magistrate. We all have different ways of coping with stress. I believe that what worked for Mr Willis was to go home, shut the door and spend what was left of the day on his own. The mayoress, if she had been with him, had her own home with her husband, son and daughter, now aged thirteen and eleven, to return to. Home for Mr Willis was now 37, Burgess Road, one of a pair of semi-detached houses he had bought in 1920. Burgess Road is on the north side of the town, with houses only on the north side which look across the cemetery to the railway station. George's sisters, Edith and Dorothy, who he called 'Diff' and 'Doff', had, I think, by then moved away from Basingstoke.

The duties of the Chief Magistrate in 1923 were, however, less demanding than they would be today. The magistrates in Basingstoke met once a month. The mayor did not always attend. The cases which came before the courts were mainly motoring offences. Exceeding the speed limit of ten miles an hour in the town's streets was the most common, some ten or twelve cases being considered each month. One driver argued that as an aviator he was used to travelling at much higher speeds. It seems that exceeding twenty miles an hour incurred a fine of £1 but if you were under that, usually about 17 miles an hour, the fine was fifteen shillings (75p). Other motoring offences included obstruction of the highway, cycling without a light, and not being in possession of a vehicle licence. The speed limit, nationally, had been raised to 20 m.p.h. as long ago as 1904, so presumably Basingstoke imposed a bye-law covering the main roads in the town centre area.

Other crimes were the use of foul language – the offending words being written on a piece of paper and passed between the magistrates – and squabbling between neighbours leading to alleged physical assault. It was difficult in these cases to obtain corroborative evidence. The latter case was usually dismissed after Mr Willis had urged all the parties to resolve their differences in a more friendly way. Keeping a dog without a licence and allowing your chimney to catch fire, for which the fine was five shillings (25p), were among the more trivial offences. One serious one was a man's 'failure to comply with a bastardy regulation'.

When the Mayor's year of office came to an end it was Mr Tigwell, who had put him forward for co-option to the Council in 1916, who moved the vote of thanks. He reminded the Council of the retiring Mayor's doubts of his ability to do the job. Now they knew that their judgement of him was correct. In fact he had turned out to be a much bigger man than they had anticipated. He had presided over the Council meetings in such a way as to allow every item before the Council to be discussed, while keeping a firm hold of the meetings so that no time was wasted. He had never missed a meeting of the full Council, and at the same time he had attended most of the committee meetings so that he fully understood the issues being discussed. He had come quite new to the work of Chief Magistrate, but those who had sat with him on the Bench felt from the start that he grasped the important duties of that office, and probably many a delinquent went away thinking not so much about the fine as as about the wise words that had fallen from the gentleman in the chair. He had also been a very approachable Mayor. No one had been afraid to go to him, and whether their trouble had been small or great they had received a patient hearing, and where he thought it wise the necessary help had been given.

In reply Mr Willis said he had expected, a year ago, to emerge from his year as Mayor with a deep sense of relief, but he was leaving with considerable regret. He thanked all those who had encouraged and supported him. He had been surprised to find that the office of Mayor did carry with it a sense of respect; that the community still looked up to the holder of it as their chief citizen. He hoped he wasn't suffering from a swollen head after all the kind things that had been said about him. He believed he was going out of office with the same size hat as he had entered it, and as a matter of fact, owing to the pressure of economic circumstances it will be found to be the same hat (Laughter).

Looking back, thirty years later, Mr Willis saw his year as mayor as a turning point in his life.

In 1923–24, in the fierce light that beats upon the Mayoral chair, I really found my feet in life and there came to me a sense of the peace which passes understanding which comes when you find your niche in life. In the Mayoralty, and in the cultivation of my other outside interests, I felt I was doing the things I was born to do, and I came to be , to some extent, the master of my own fate.

In moving the vote of thanks Mr Tigwell did not forget to remind Mr Willis that he had been a bachelor mayor during a leap year. 'We know that the fair sex have certain privileges in leap year, and I believe those privileges were made use of by some, unfortunately without success.'

Little evidence of their efforts remains. Among the papers kept by the family are a poem signed by 'Eva Sigh'! and a letter, written on 10 March, addressed 'Dear Mr Mayor', congratulating him on his engagement, asking when the wedding day was going to be, and saying that they understood that ladies with hazel eyes made good wives, signed by the Munday family. When I first saw this I felt sure it was genuine. Albert Munday's daughter and I were both Trustees of the Basingstoke Charity. She was also a client of mine. A lovely lady whom I couldn't imagine indulging in this sort of joke. It was later when I read the Town Clerk's remarks and saw that Albert Munday was a councillor at the time, I had to accept that, having been written less than two weeks after 29 February, the letter was not serious – a simple example of the traps that lie in wait for the unwary historian.

In some people's memories, there seems to be a romantic link between Mr Willis and the lady who was the Town Clerk's secretary at the time. This lady was helping Mr Willis in 1930 by typing captions for the exhibits in the new museum. Did she have hazel eyes? Mr Willis never did marry. The electoral roll of 1973 shows the lady in question, still a spinster, still living in Sarum Hill. Mrs Goddard, who was housekeeper to Mr Willis, remembers her as a friend of his but is sure there was no romantic attachment between them. Mr Willis's name is also linked with that of another lady who at one time worked in the shop and who, it is said, rejected him in favour of another man whom she married and with whom she moved away from Basingstoke. The truth, I am sure, will never be known. It is difficult to see how family life could have been fitted in to the extraordinarily busy life he enjoyed. Although he became so involved with Basingstoke's schools, always ready to help and advise young people, he may have been afraid of the personal responsibility of parenthood.

During his year as mayor, Mr Willis was elected a governor of both Queen Mary's School and the Girls' High School. Having become a governor of the Girls' High School in 1923 he was elected chairman of the governors in the following year, serving in that capacity until 1960. The endearing qualities for which he was to be remembered at the school were a smiling shyness, generosity, delight in being amongst young people, a certain old fashioned courtesy.

Mr Willis had become a governor of his old school, Queen Mary's, before he joined the board of the Girls' High School. He was never chairman but in February 1924 he presided, as mayor, at the annual prize giving. We must be grateful to the editor of the *Hants & Berks Gazette* that the speech he made was reported in full.

Mr Willis started by remembering the first day he came into the school – a good deal more shy and retiring than he was now (Laughter) and, coming up to the present, he said he had heard someone at the back of the hall say 'I suppose he is going to give us the same old stodgy stuff about trying to be good citizens.' (Laughter) Well he was not going to. He did not want to say much about the work of the school but he did want to say how learning Latin had enabled him to decipher the inscriptions on tombstones which he had seen when taken on a visit to Westminster Abbey. Mr Willis then went on to develop his main theme that knowledge should be acquired for the enrichment of life and the part that hobbies played in making life enjoyable.

He told the boys of his own early days. 'My Saturday mornings used to be given up to homework and of all the dreary subjects I found mathematics was the worst.' (Laughter) 'But on Saturday afternoons I and another boy explored the neighbourhood. We used to take long walks, coming back with wet feet, very muddy and untidy, but with a sense of having done something. We made it our duty to know every stream and pond in the neighbourhood.' He went on to speak of the chalk pits they explored and the churches they visited. 'There was one church the door to the tower of which could be very easily forced with the blade of a knife. We got a tremendous view from that tower. I won't tell you which church it was.' (Laughter) As Mr Willis recalled the places he had visited as a boy, he also spoke of all the extra knowledge he had since acquired – of his understanding of flints, of being able to identify wild flowers, of learning of the historical events associated with different places – and how he enjoyed these places even more than he had done as a boy.

Towards the end of his talk Mr Willis forecast that someday Basingstoke would have a museum, and the town would look for curators from boys of the Grammar School – those who had made a study of botany, geology, beetles, butterflies and birds. There was also a need to take photographs. The countryside in the neighbourhood was changing very rapidly, and in fifty years' time photographs taken now would be interesting and valuable. My own memories of school days in the 1930s was that visiting dignitaries gave us the old stodgy stuff about citizenship which Mr Willis avoided. His talk must have been electrifying.

A month after his term of office as mayor ended, Mr Willis was one of forty men who met to consider a proposal to form a Queen Mary's Old Boys' Association. The headmaster was invited to be president. George Willis was one of the fourteen old boys and staff who were elected as vice-presidents. The first dinner was arranged for March 1925. From then on George rarely failed to attend these annual functions.

When a former mayor, Mr Sterry Wallis, died during Mr Willis's year of office, he took over some of the positions Mr Wallis had held. This included chairman of the Municipal Charities Trustees and chairman of the Aldworth Trustees. He had not previously been a Trustee of the Aldworth Foundation but at the first meeting he attended Canon Boustead, the vicar of Basingstoke, proposed that he should be elected chairman. Both posts were of special interest in that he was taking his place in the long line of citizens who, through the centuries, had administered these charities, each generation caring for their own people.

At the next meeting of the Aldworth Foundation, held in the Town Hall at 11 30 a.m. on Tuesday 1 July 1925, one boy was included in the list of successful candidates for the Aldworth Foundation scholarship who the masters at Queen Mary's School were to consider a tiresome, unruly, troublemaker for whom they could see no future. He was to leave the school without any scholastic qualification. Against all the odds he achieved worldwide fame, something no Basingstoker had ever done. As chairman of the Aldworth Trustees, Mr Willis had to meet all the Aldworth Foundation scholars at the end of each term to receive their school report. In an article published in *Hampshire, the county magazine*, in 1962, John Arlott described the meetings he had with Mr Willis.

When I held an Aldworth Scholarship, I had to present myself at the end of each term at a local solicitor's office, to receive my report, with appropriate comment, from the trustee of the Foundation, who was George Willis. As I came uneasily in, he would stand up from behind an imposing desk completely out of character with the slim, small-boned man, with his sensitive, almost delicate face, and well-worn, but never shabby, grey suit. He would smile shyly, ask me to sit down, and unfold my report with the happy, anticipatory air of one who had not seen it before and was confident of my having done well. Religious instruction, Geography, History, English, Latin, French, Arithmetic – a commendatory 'Yes, yes' or 'Good' or, though rarely, 'Oh, yes, first, well done, I am glad'. But then came Geometry, Algebra, Chemistry, Physics, Art and finally, hours of detention and the Headmaster's verdict on my conduct! From bad to worse. How we suffered for one another. I hated to distress him; he did not want to grumble. I felt intuitively that, despite all the evidence to the contrary before his eyes, he wanted, in his charity, to believe I was a good boy. Somehow – and we became, I feel, very fond of one another, in the process – we comforted one another with the mutual belief that next term's report would be better. It never was; but it never roused a harsh word from my predecessor and trustee.

I found a letter in the Hampshire Record Office which John Arlott wrote to Mr Willis in 1962. John signed the letter he had typed and added, in his own handwriting, 'Many thanks for so much kindness over all these years – and for the foundation of such success as I have had.'

Now that his year as mayor was over Mr Willis had more time to pursue some of his other interests. He was a vice-president of the Mechanics' Institute but would not be persuaded to be president. At the 1925 AGM it was reported that membership was 271, against 263 in 1923. Mr Willis noticed that extreme economy had been exercised by the Committee in charge of the library. The reporter, who wrote that Mr Willis had not mentioned this altogether in a spirit of congratulation, was, I am sure, quoting Mr Willis's own words. The billiard's room was popular, and *Webster's Dictionary* was being well used. It was assumed this was for solving crossword puzzles.

There was more time for John Ellaway and himself to explore for fossils and prehistoric sites. I am reasonably certain that the two men had by now been joined by Mr Rainbow in their search for the artefacts of early man. The cash book of the Mechanics' Institute shows Mr

Rainbow as being a member as early as 1917. There was also more time to talk to friends about Basingstoke's more recent history. One of these friends was George Woodman, the retired chemist of Odiham, who could remember going to the Willis saddlery firm in Basingstoke to have a length of string made for his kite. He had kept a diary every day since 1862, and contributed articles on Basingstoke's past to the local paper, sometimes with the assistance of Mr Willis.

It was during 1924 that Horace Carey opened an outfitter's shop at 23 Church Street. Mr Willis was one of a small group of local business people who gave him financial assistance to get started. The family do not know how their father first met Mr Willis. It may have been at the Mechanics' Institute, but it is also probable that they were introduced by mutual friends. Horace Carey worshipped at the Congregational Church which so many of the business community attended. He was twenty years younger than Mr Willis and at that time the two men may have have had little in common. Horace was a member of the Congregational Church football team which played teams representing other churches. In later years he helped organise the Basingstoke Corinthians, a well-known local football team. Although some friends remember seeing Mr Willis skating at Hackwood Park in hard winters, it is difficult to imagine him taking part in team games. Horace Carey's father was a railwayman who was a founder member of the Basingstoke Co-operative Society. This was started by a group of railwaymen pooling their savings to buy a truck-load of coal which they shared out between themselves.

Mr Willis's period of office as an alderman expired at the end of 1926. So did that of Alderman George Pheby, a member of the Labour Party and a former mayor. A Council meeting was held to elect two aldermen to fill the vacancies. Both the retiring aldermen were eligible for re-election. The mayor's name was one of the six proposed. He and Mr T.C. Chesterfield received five votes each, Mr Willis and Mr Pheby four votes and the other two candidates one vote each. Mr Chesterfield stood up and said that he did not think he could spare the time to be an alderman but was persuaded against resigning. He was elected mayor the following year. Mr Willis moved into the public seats and sat there for a short time. He heard the mayor say that he hoped the outgoing aldermen would be back on the Council fairly soon. Mr Willis then left. It was going to be seven years before he next had a seat on the Council. Happily, these were not going to be lean years.

Chapter Four
1926–1933 Museum Curator

'... this Museum is Mr Willis's baby and without Mr Willis there would have been no Museum in Basingstoke ...'

John Arlott's opinion was that Mr Willis regarded his failure to be re-elected as alderman as a sign that Basingstoke no longer wanted him on the Council. Certainly he did not seek re-election. The political scene in Basingstoke was changing as the monopoly of the town's business community was being eroded by working-class people who were members of the Labour Party. Although he was regarded as a mild Liberal, Mr Willis always stood as an Independent. His only wish was to serve the town he loved. The manoeuvres of party politics were of no interest to him.

There were always other ways in which he could serve the town. The Mechanics' Institute, which had been opened with so much enthusiasm in 1869, was now in trouble. When members met for the AGM on 5 March 1927, they learnt that it was in danger of going bankrupt. The decision was made to offer the premises to the Council for use as a free library and a museum. The officers elected at that AGM were the same people Mr Willis had been associated with during his years on the Council. Albert Munday succeeded Mr Willis's old friend William Buckland as President. John Ellaway was secretary and treasurer. The committee included R. Webber the motor engineer, A.G. Wood the organist, and H. Carey who was to become one of Mr Willis's closest friends in the future. The town council accepted the offer of the building and established a library on the ground floor. John Ellaway was appointed honorary librarian. The upper floor was left empty. Its potential use to house a museum depended on money becoming available to set it up.

When he was mayor there had been an exchange of letters between the regional secretary of Rotary and Mr Willis, with the secretary suggesting to Mr Willis how he could form a Rotary Club in Basingstoke. The letters do not show whether the initiative came from Rotary or Mr Willis. In September 1927 Mr Willis was one of the nine founder members of the Rotary Club of Basingstoke. The founder president was the Minister of the Congregational Church, the Rev. S. Stanley. Mr Willis was vice-president. These members, with sixteen others, became the Charter Members on 7 November. A photograph of Mr Willis which must have been taken at about this time, because he is wearing the Rotary badge in his lapel, shows him looking remarkably young for his 50 years.

Meetings were held on Mondays at 1 p.m. at Darracott's Cafe Royal. This meant a short walk for Mr Willis along London Street to where it is crossed by New Street. The building was originally the *Three Tuns* public house, and is now the offices of a firm of estate agents. Lunch, with waitress service, cost one shilling and sixpence (7.5p in decimal coinage). Meetings were also held at the Devon Café, which advertised luncheons and dainty teas.

At one of the meetings, held in the first year, Mr Willis set out his ideas on what a museum should be and how it could contribute to the quality of life in the town. A museum was not, he said,

> *a sort of dustbin into which folk relegate all those things knocking about the house which their conscience will not allow them to destroy. And it is not intended merely to be a place of shelter on a rainy day. It is entirely dynamic in its character and not static.*

He went on to speak of the associations we have with physical objects.

> *Our forefathers have lived here for infinite generations and we inherit the tradition they have created. That tradition is often associated with concrete objects. We can see products of their handicrafts and their thought. As these things accumulate in a museum we can rightly rejoice over them and feel proud of them. [For 1500 years] our fathers have shouldered the civic and municipal duties of their time and have handed on to us Basingstoke as it is known today. It is our duty to develop this civic tradition and to instill in the minds of the present inhabitants the idea that they are citizens of no mean city.*

Next to his pride in being a Basingstoker, which influenced all his actions, was George's belief in education.

> *A museum must concern itself with education, particularly the education of the younger people. Where there is an adequate and ordered display of specimens the interest of the child's mind is attracted and led on from one thing to another until he is led to see the halo of romance in it all.*

A museum would have many parts to play. It could keep up to date a permanent record of the district's vanishing archaeological features. It could exhibit a record of the local flora, fauna and geological features. It could be a home to the the town's ancient documents which, kept in the muniment room of the Town Hall, were never on show to the public. There should come back to Basingstoke the remains of a Roman house found in May Street. As for flint instruments the hillsides in the district were simply strewn thick with the remains of earliest humankind.

The Mechanics' Institute had offered its buildings to the Council. Its upper room was admirably suited for a museum. The obstacle to establishing a museum there was the cost of fitting it up. The cost of showcases would probably be about £600, the same cost, in 1928, as an average-size house or four popular cars. Mr Willis asked his fellow Rotarians to help promote the realisation of his scheme.

When the ground floor of the Mechanics' Institute was opened as a free library by Sir William Portal, whose uncle had laid the foundation stone for the building, he expressed his approval to the concept of a museum on the upper floor. He mentioned his own interest in the archaeology and botany, with which Hampshire is so richly endowed, and his having had the honour, on more than one occasion, of being president of the Hampshire Field Club. He felt he need scarcely remind those present that the borough had someone eminently suited to assist in this project, in the person of Mr Willis. The museum could not come into being, however, until there were cases in which the exhibits could be displayed, and he appealed to friends in Basingstoke or outside it to assist in supplying these necessary cases.

Mr Willis had taken the opportunity – on the day the library was opened – of setting up a small exhibition of some of the archaeological finds that he, Mr Ellaway and Mr Rainbow had collected. The newspaper report implied, unfortunately, that these were their total collection which Mr Willis had given to the town. Mr Willis lost no time in writing to the editor.

I feel there are certain inferences to be drawn from your report that, while approximating to the truth, are not as exact as you would desire. It would probably surprise my colleagues to learn that I had blandly presented their property to the town. Your comments, however, are in the nature of intelligent anticipation.

He then went on to confirm that as soon as suitable premises became available he and his friends intended to give their collections to found a museum, and that they had already found ten times the amount of material shown in the temporary exhibition. Mr Willis ended his letter by setting out his idea that a museum could encourage all lovers of nature to set up and maintain an exhibition of the flora and wild life of the district.

Two years went by before the money became available and it was Mr Allnutt, who had been mayor during the war when Mr Willis was first on the Council, who made the museum possible. In a letter Mr Willis wrote me in 1964 he explained how this came about.

Dear Mr Wren,

I have read your draft with great pleasure & was very interested in the association of the photos with the relevant subject matter.

There are two trifling inaccuracies & one that I should like to see corrected. This refers to the establishment of the museum & its connection with Mr Allnutt. The whole initiative leading to the establishment came from Mr A & not from the council. Mr A was Mayor 1916–1919 & the Museum was formed – at his instigation – in 1930. He one day came to me & said he was prepared to lay down £500 if the Council would do the same.

The Council fortunately had a Town Clerk interested in education & the Council agreed. So I was given £1000 & a big room & told to get on with it. It is sometimes embarrassing to be asked to practise what you have been preaching. However I had a very happy year in preparation & many subsequently in running it. Naturally I retain great respect for Mr A & should like him to have all the credit he deserves for his positive action.

Yours sincerely, G.W. Willis

The Grand Theatre in Basingstoke was showing the film *One Romantic Night*, starring Lilian Gish in her first talking picture, when the museum was opened in January 1931. Three people who were to speak at the opening of the museum were unable to attend because of illness. The Earl of Malmesbury was asked, at very short notice, to open the museum in the place of Sir William Portal who was ill. The chairman of the Library and Museums Committee, Mrs Weston, had gone to visit her sick mother and the deputy-mayor, Councillor Dallimore, was unable to be there because of the death of his father. Both Sir William Portal and Mrs Weston had written expressing their appreciation of Mr Allnutt's generosity and the hard work put in by Mr Willis and Mr Ellaway to get the museum ready.

Rev. S. Wing, speaking in place of Mrs Weston, described the events leading up to the establishment of the museum, referring to the gigantic task of collecting and classifying the objects of interest for display. This work had been carried out with such zeal and enthusiasm by Mr Willis and Mr Ellaway, for whom this must be a red letter day. The Curator of the Reading Museum then congratulated the Mayor on what had been achieved and advised keeping the museum as a local museum. When the Mayor asked Mr Willis to describe the scheme of the exhibition he said, 'This museum is Mr Willis's baby, and without Mr Willis there would be no museum in Basingstoke.' Mr Willis said,

The aim of the museum is to explain Basingstoke. Starting with fossils illustrating life existing in the area before man arrived and going on to relics of prehistoric man, continuing with artefacts and documents which as you walked around the room told the story from Roman times to the present day, photographs also being used for the last hundred years.

The only periods of the town's history for which there were few exhibits to display were Saxon and Early Medieval. Mr Willis acknowledged his debt to the band of local archaeologists he had known in his youth. He was glad to see two of them, Mr Attwood and Mr Woodman, were present. He also mentioned Mr Rainbow – the third member of the fraternity – who had given not only a third of the prehistoric material but was responsible for the very fine contour map at the end of the room, which involved months and months of work. Mr Willis said that the year he had spent with his colleagues preparing for the opening of the museum had been the busiest year of his life, having to work even harder than when he was mayor.

The meeting ended with tea in the Reading Room of the Library downstairs. George Woodman, by then 86, went home and wrote in his diary that this had been a red letter day. Both Mr Woodman and Mr Allnutt died the following year.

The week after the opening the *Hants & Berks Gazette* published a letter from a friend of Mr Rainbow, complaining that the speakers at the opening ceremony had not given him the credit he deserved. We found little information about Mr Rainbow. A letter of his, published in the *Hants & Berks Gazette* in 1927, reporting the sighting of a rare butterfly – the marbled white butterfly (*Melanagria galathea*) – shows that he was as knowledgeable about wildlife as he was about archaeology. He was very deaf so, if he found conversation difficult, his presence may not have been noticed as much as that of Mr Willis and Mr Ellaway.

During the year the museum was being assembled these 'three men of vision' were joined by a part-time colleague, Geoffrey Civil, a school master from Gosport. As he explained in a letter he wrote me in 1970,

> You may probably know that I was the final addition to the famous trio, Messrs Willis, Ellaway & Rainbow, who worked so successfully in establishing the Basingstoke Museum, my apprenticeship dating from about 1930. Since that time Mr Willis has been my mentor and close friend. At his suggestion I, and my family, always refer to him as 'Uncle George'.
>
> Throughout the years I have spent practically every school holiday at Basingstoke enjoying the greatest interest of my life – archaeology! Thursday afternoons and all day Sundays doing research work in the field with Uncle George and long hours every night of the week working in the Curator's room at the Museum. He was pleased to refer to me as 'an honorary member of the staff of the Basingstoke Museum' It is only natural that through such long and close contact I was able to observe aspects of his character unknown to the public at large. Basingstoke may at the present or in the future produce someone equally as worthy; but Basingstoke will never produce, in devotion and dedication to the service of his native town, a son more worthy than George W. Willis. You do well to honour him.

Another disciple of the same period was Stephen Usherwood.

> Mr Willis was my first friend in Basingstoke, when, in 1931, I came to Queen Mary's as my first post after graduating at Oxford. He showed me the records of the enclosures of the open fields round Basingstoke in huge bound volumes in the vaults of the Town Hall – most valuable documents for the economic historian and very little known.

In his letter Stephen went on to ask me to draw attention to the generous work of Mrs Weston, the first woman mayor of Basingstoke, in building up the library and museum. 'She was a great admirer of Mr Willis and shared his enthusiasm for the museum and the preservation of Basingstoke history.' Stephen had married Mrs Weston's daughter, Hazel, who had been head girl at the Girls' High School. Their marriage must have given particular pleasure to Mr Willis.

The newspaper report on the opening of the museum ended with the message: 'We are asked to state that the Museum will be open to the public each day from 2 p.m. until 9 p.m.' Mr Willis had signalled his intention of being available to the public as much as possible, going round to the museum each day after he closed the shop. He had a gift for sharing his enthusiasm with other people. Youngsters would call in the museum in the evening, after school, hoping he would be there to describe the exhibits and explain their significance. When he addressed the annual prize-giving meetings of the schools where he was a governor, he would talk of Basingstoke's past. He was always as ready to learn as he was to teach. For him teaching and learning went hand in hand. At the end of 1931 he wrote to the paper, drawing attention to the poor attendance at the lectures being given on Tuesday evenings at the Town Hall on the subject 'Delight in books'. Perhaps it was the eminence of the lecturer, Dr Thomas Moult that was scaring the public away.

As a fact, the lectures have an easy, conversational and racy style and pleasantly combine entertainment with sound instruction and I feel that many of my friends are missing something they would thoroughly enjoy.

These lectures may have been arranged by the Workers Educational Association. Both Mr Willis and Mr Ellaway were lifelong supporters of the WEA.

Running in parallel with Mr Willis's effort to attract the public into the museum was his concern to obtain more exhibits. He published a list in the paper of appropriate articles the museum would be pleased to acquire. It covered more than twenty categories of all kinds – the Basingstoke canal, newspapers, coins, books, household utensils, costumes, maps, local records of the Great War, flora and fauna, to make a random selection. He argued that by donating items of historical interest to the museum the donors would be assured that their treasures would be put in a place of safety and that they would be made available for everyone to enjoy. For years he reported to the paper on the museum's recent acquisitions. One of the museum's oddest exhibits, but one for which it became well known, was 'the giant spider of Basingstoke' which was found in 1932 in a crate of bananas. This can no longer be seen, thrown out, no doubt, by some later curator.

The year after the museum opened Mr O.G.S. Crawford, 'the eminent archaeologist', as Mr Willis described him, wrote an appreciation, published in the *Hants & Berks Gazette*.

The Basingstoke Museum is a good museum. I cannot think of a better one, and I have seen many. There is about it an atmosphere of helpfulness, that puts one in the right frame of mind. Who could be unmoved by the portrait of 'our oldest resident' chipping away at his flint in front of a palaeolithic fire. There are not, as so often, too many exhibits; the labels are concise and legible and written in really good English; they 'put their message across' effectively.

Mr Crawford next mentioned the excellent map of the Basingstoke district, the geological model of the Basingstoke area and the label, attached to cases, 'For further reading consult the lending library downstairs'. He then went on to take the reader on a tour of the museum, the cases of prehistoric remains, Roman artefacts from villas once inhabited not by Romans, but by prosperous native Britons, and so on through the centuries, ending with exhibits of Victorian Basingstoke. Compared with the abundance of medieval records, mostly in the form of documents, there were few traces of Saxon occupation in the town. The report ended by acknowledging that the museum 'is the creation of three residents who have, with great public spirit, thrown their own collections into the common pool'.

Osbert Guy Stanhope Crawford, CBE, was a man who Mr Willis probably admired and respected more than anyone else he knew. Nine years younger than Mr Willis, he was born in Bombay, the son of a judge, came home to attend his father's old school, Marlborough and then went on to Keble College, Oxford where he obtained a degree in geography. At the outbreak of World War 1 he was in the Sudan doing archaeological excavation. After joining the infantry he transferred to the Royal Flying Corps as an observer. While a prisoner of war, after being shot down, he wrote his first book on archaeology. In 1920 he was appointed as the first Archaeology Officer of the Ordnance Survey, a position he held until the end of World War 2. He was responsible for producing the ordnance survey map of Roman Britain, was a pioneer in the use of photography in archaeological research, and founder and editor of the quarterly journal *Antiquity*. Mr Willis had almost certainly met him through the Hampshire Field Club. Mr Crawford had the reputation of being unconventional in his dress, wearing shorts before they had become acceptable and, as one obituary stated, 'not suffering fools gladly'. His criticisms, both in conversation and in the editorial column of *Antiquity*, made him very unpopular in some quarters. Praise from Mr Crawford, therefore, was highly valued.

The exhibition of local wild flowers was probably started the year before the museum opened. A white-painted wooden stand was made, with shelves drilled with holes into which fitted test tubes, each containing a single specimen of a wild flower, labelled to give both its Latin name and its popular name. This stand was fixed to the wall at the foot of the stairs that went up to the museum, so that visitors to both the museum and the library could see what they might expect to find in the countryside at that time of the year and be able to identify the flowers they found. These specimens needed to be regularly renewed, as flowers of different seasons appeared and earlier ones died off. A letter from the curators to the local paper, asking for the public's assistance in finding examples, brought forth a stinging rebuke from the secretary of the Society for the Protection of Wild Flowers and Plants. He read, with dismay, the appeal made by Messrs Willis and Ellaway which is 'a direct, though unintended, encouragement of vandalism and destruction, for presumably the rarer the plant the bigger its welcome. True nature lovers do not dig up plants for exhibition ... There are so many plants on the verge of extinction that every effort must be made to discourage these exhibitions of plant life.'

The writer of the letter had clearly underestimated the calibre of the two men he was dealing with. Their reply, the following week, noted with regret the dismay they had unwittingly caused, especially as they were in entire sympathy with the good intentions – as distinct from the statements – of the correspondent.

> But we have to declare ourselves entirely unrepentant, and we feel that the extravagant character of the criticism robs it of any useful purpose. Strange as it may seem to Mr Harding (secretary of the SPWFP), our effort has been to run the exhibition on correct scientific lines, wherein every flower from the commonest to the rarer, has an equal place, inasmuch as every species, to the real botanist, is equally wonderful.

They entirely agreed that plants should not be dug up, and,

> to associate the 'digging up of plants' with anything that we have done or invited or suggested is preposterous nonsense. The actual result of our show has been an awakened interest in the glory of their countryside on the part of many who previously had little or no idea of the beauty and variety of nature around them, and the expressions of appreciation that have reached us have been both ample reward for the work involved and a full justification of the principle of a local exhibition.

Their mastery of logic and the English language made Mr Willis and Mr Ellaway a formidable match for anyone who disagreed with their views. The exhibition of wild flowers continued to be a popular feature of the museum. It was still there when Margaret and I came to Basingstoke in 1962 but was discontinued a few years later.

Mr Willis never allowed his involvement with the museum and other interests to divert him from ensuring that the firm of G.W. Willis & Son was in good shape. While he concentrated on the repair side of the business, and looking after clocks in the big houses around Basingstoke, the shop attracted people looking for presents. Although there were other jewellers in the town, many friends have told me that his shop was the first one they went to. Two sisters remember their excitement when they were given gold watches on their twenty-first birthdays. Mary Felgate, who was a lifelong friend of George's niece Barbara, remembers his shop as

... a treasure house full of beautiful things. It was absolutely stacked with every kind of thing that you could want to buy. Silver things and gold things, large and small, masses of watches, necklaces, rings, pendants. There were expensive things, but mostly they were things that people could buy for special Christmas and birthday presents. He did all the watch mending. You could look through past the counter and see him and Mr Adams sitting up by the work bench.

The scene outside the shop had changed over the years with the growth of car ownership. People who a few years earlier were going for day outings in groups on charabancs were now buying their own cars, as the prices had been reduced by mass production. Traffic from London was again passing through the town's main streets on its way to Southampton or the West Country. A Mr Clark, speaking to the Rotary Club in 1930, described the centre of the town as it would have appeared to anyone passing the Willis shop as they came up Wote Street.

Continuing up this steep and narrow road we reach the Market Place with its curious Town Hall and cast iron clock tower. Traffic immediately confronts us – traffic of every description, from enormous stacks of milk churns on wheels to the normal small car. Obviously the road is too small for the traffic.

At times the traffic may have moved as slowly as it had done when there was a 10 m.p.h. speed limit in Basingstoke, even more slowly when motorists found themselves behind cattle being driven to the market or pigs and sheep going to the slaughter houses which some butchers had behind their shops. Basingstokers who were around in those days have memories of being pinned against the iron railings, which were then a feature of the town, as cattle passed by. Most of these railings were to go to feed the war effort in World War 2, changing the appearance of the town.

When a by-pass was opened the next year, diverting through traffic around the south of the town, Mr Willis and Mr Ellaway joined forces, as they often did, to send a letter to the *Hants & Berks Gazette*, pointing out that the new road followed the line of a much older road.

> *As far as the part [of the by-pass] from the Stag and Hounds on the Winchester Road along Pack Lane to Skippets Lane is concerned, this line of roadway will be resuming rather than attaining its place in the great highway from east to west across Hampshire. It coincides for this specified distance with the line of the Harrow Way, the most important of the old Hampshire trackways, whose precise origin must be assigned to prehistoric times.*

After seven years had passed since Mr Willis played any part in making decisions on the town's administration, friends persuaded him to stand in the 1933 municipal election. The results justified their confidence. Mr Willis came top of the poll with 2083 votes. Only one other candidate topped the 2000 mark. The four candidates elected included one member of the Labour Party. Three of the five candidates who were not successful were also members of the Labour Party, and another one, with a double-barrelled name, had, each week during the campaign, paid for an advertisement, with a photograph of himself, to be put in the local paper. Mr Willis stood as an Independent. I cannot imagine him going round the streets canvassing. When the results were declared by the mayor standing outside the Town Hall, Mr Willis said that for the last fortnight he had lived in a pleasant atmosphere of friendly greeting, and he hoped he might enjoy his part as councillor as well.

Chapter Five

1933–1940 Alderman and JP

'It is for this Council to have an eye to the future, especially now that we are, I hope, on the eve of a period of development in building.'

Some men and women have the urge constantly to find new tasks to accomplish, new worlds to explore. That was not the nature of Mr Willis. His work at the shop, his role as curator of the museum, his service to his town as a councillor, a Rotarian, a trustee for the town's charities, a governor of the town's schools satisfied all his needs. He was never bored. He continued to spend his leisure hours – those precious Sundays and Thursday afternoons – exploring the countryside around Basingstoke, searching for more evidence of the activities of our ancestors, understanding the geology of the district, finding new specimens of wild flowers. The thrill of finding new sites that were inhabited in the distant past, of handling primitive instruments that no one else had touched for thousands of years, never grew less. As he translated the Latin of ancient documents he found in the Council's muniments room his knowledge of Basingstoke's history grew in depth.

Communicating the knowledge he acquired became a major activity for himself and Mr Ellaway. In August 1934 Mr Willis gave a talk to the Rotary Club on 'Old Basingstoke'. In June the following year Mr Ellaway spoke to the club, and later in that year Mr Willis was in Preston Candover at the village hall, speaking to the Women's Institute on 'Preston Candover through the Ages'. All these talks were fully reported in the *Hants & Berks Gazette*. I was intrigued to read the report of a talk Mr Willis gave to Rotary on 'Geological Exhibits at the Museum' in March 1935. It was given at short notice, due to the illness of the appointed speaker, and ended with Mr Willis quoting a piece of poetry about the nautilus, written by the author and former scientist, Oliver Wendell Holmes. My copy of *The Autocrat at the Breakfast Table*, Holmes' best known work, has slept undisturbed on my bookshelves for many years. This piece of poetry was from some other work. How was Mr Willis able to produce these lines of poetry? Had he read them and remembered them, or did his friend John Ellaway, the 'omnivorous reader' as he called him, supply him with the quotation? Mr Willis must have read a good deal. He had shelves full of books in his homes and probably read late into the evening but this poem must be from a little known work, and certainly not a technical work on one of his chosen subjects.

Early in December1934 Mr Willis received a letter from the Clerk of the Peace requesting him to attend 'at the next Quarter Sessions to be held at the Castle of Winchester on Monday the 14th day of January 1935 to take the Oath of Allegiance and the Judicial Oath' enabling him to act as a magistrate. Mr Willis was appointed both as a Borough Magistrate and a County Magistrate. As a magistrate he was liable to sit on the Bench at the Town Hall on Tuesday mornings for the Borough Petty Sessions and on Wednesday mornings for the Basingstoke Petty Sessional Division. The latter court covered offences committed in the villages around Basingstoke. His fellow magistrates for Borough Petty Sessions were nearly all fellow tradesmen and members of the Council, but the chairman of the other court, as listed in *Kelly's Directory* for 1939, was General Sir George Darell Jeffreys, KCB, KCVO, CMG. Charles Chute, of the Vyne, was vice-chairman and the other members included the Duke of Wellington, Mr Jervoise of Herriard, a major-general and brigadier-general. In 1939 Mr Willis was one of the few magistrates serving in both courts.

One disappointment my wife and I have had, in researching the life of Mr Willis, has been our failure to contact any one with memories of Mr Willis as a magistrate. I wrote to the firm of Lamb Brooks, solicitors, whose senior partner, 'Bobby' Brooks was clerk to the court in Mr Willis's time, the week in which Mr Brooks died. The only account we found was in an article by John Arlott.

The only independent on the Council; and shrewd as ever, yet he never seems cross: only sometimes, as a magistrate, when someone comes before him for an offence not just illegal – he has a gentle belief that people can be illegal without being wicked – but an offence which he thinks is mean: then his indignation flares – I remember his scorn of a woman who had stolen some flowers off a grave: it was so strong and just and flaming.

The cases that came before the Borough Petty Sessions were no different from those the Court had dealt with when he was mayor and chief magistrate eleven years earlier. In March fines were handed out to a motorist without an off-side and a rear light, another one driving a car without a licence and a cyclist without a rear light. An Egyptian student, working at the Thorneycroft & Co. works, was fined five shillings (25p) for having aided and abetted a juvenile to carry more than one person on a bicycle which was not constructed or adapted for that purpose. The defendant said he did not know it was wrong. Coming from a country where such a practice was normal that may have been true.

The cases that came before the Petty Sessional Division were similar. Motoring offences still formed the bulk of the cases tried. Being a JP was not a very onerous responsibility. Mr Willis only occasionally attended the court hearings, and as these were held at the Town Hall just across the road from his shop he lost no time in going to them.

Basingstoke was still a law-abiding town. Every evening after the shop shut the caretaker who lived upstairs came down to fix wooden shutters over the windows. When they were in position a bar was fixed across them , secured in place with a padlock, but Mr Willis never asked for this to be locked. He never expected the shop to be burgled. A smash and grab raid did occur once. Mr Willis was woken early one Sunday morning to be told that a shutter had been broken off, the window broken with a brick and a tray of rings and watches taken. On another occasion a man came into the shop and asked to see some diamond rings. He was shown a tray of rings. Having distracted the assistant's attention, he snatched up the tray, ran off to a waiting car and got away. Only two losses in the 85 years between his father founding the firm and Mr Willis selling it was a good record and justified his policy of not insuring the business.

The museum seemed more vulnerable to crime than the shop. Just after Christmas 1934 one of the cases in the museum was broken open and a scale model of a Midland Railway locomotive stolen. The magazine *Model Engineer* had a notice in the next edition asking if any of its readers could assist in locating the model. A year later a collection of valuable coins was stolen. It was thought that the thieves had hidden themselves in the building before closing time. The police made widespread inquiries concerning a motor car which had been seen leaving the neighbourhood some time after the museum had been closed. Interviewed by reporters Mr Willis said he did not think the thieves had any expert knowledge of coins. They had taken large gold and silver pieces, leaving much older coins which were, presumably, more valuable.

As early as 1923, in his acceptance speech as mayor, Mr Willis had said that Basingstoke needed a planning policy to control its physical development. Now in 1937 he moved that the Council take into consideration the preparation of a Town Planning Scheme for the borough, and that the Finance and General Purposes Committee be asked to report thereon. This plan would only apply to areas likely to be used for building, and would give the community the opportunity to indicate, to some extent, the way in which these areas should be developed. Mr Willis said,

> It was for this Council, as trustees of the public weal, to have an eye to the future, especially now that they were [he hoped] on the eve of a period of development in building. Having regard also to the increasing problems created by motor traffic and the provision of roads for it, it was more than ever necessary that the Council should consider the adoption of such a scheme.

He explained the procedure which would have to be adopted for the preparation of a plan which would have to be submitted to the Ministry of Health (a public enquiry). This would not involve a considerable expenditure, but although he

> was loath to entertain the idea of borrowing small sums for any purpose whatever, having regard to the fact that almost all the advantages of a town planning scheme would mature in future years, and would be much more valuable fifty years hence than it would be immediately [he thought] the costs in this matter should be covered by loan.

Mr Musselwhite seconded the motion, and it was agreed without further discussion. It is clear that Mr Willis had carefully prepared his case, so that his fellow councillors would have had difficulty in rejecting his arguments.

Mr Willis saw very clearly that Basingstoke would grow and change, although he could not have envisaged the development that would take place at the end of his life. Time and time again, over many years, in speeches and articles, different people had drawn attention to Basingstoke's natural advantages as a place for development. Situated between London and Southampton, with good rail and road links, this was the place where new factories should be sited, and new industries developed. Eli Lilly, the American pharmaceutical company, did in fact build a factory in Basingstoke, just to the north of the railway line – their first overseas development – in that year (1937).

There is a delightful story, which various people told us, illustrating Mr Willis's reaction to councillors who joined in the debate without having anything worthwhile to contribute. It may be apocryphal but it is worth telling. Before leaving the shop to go to a council meeting Mr Willis would strap several watches, which he had in for repair, to his arm. When he lost interest in the discussion, he turned up his sleeve, took off one of the watches, produced tools and his watchmaker's eye-glass, and proceeded to repair the watch. If the story is true I am sure he was still able to follow the debate while working.

Mr Willis regained his position as alderman in 1937. He had been re-elected as councillor the year before, coming second to Mr W.H. Musselwhite who was mayor elect. Towards the end of 1937 Alderman Chesterfield, who had received one vote more than Mr Willis in the election of aldermen back in 1926, was finding the pressure of running his business and serving on the council too great. He resigned and Mr Willis was elected in his place.

1937 was also the year when, in May, Basingstoke celebrated the coronation of King George VI and Queen Elizabeth. As on earlier occasions Mr Willis was involved, this time on the fund-raising committee. Unlike earlier occasions when the day ended with music in the Market Place, there was now music and dancing in the Memorial Park. Six months later the Council elected Councillor Edith Weston as mayor, the first time in the history of the town that a woman had held that position. Only two women have since held office as mayor of Basingstoke and by coincidence the last one to do so was Councillor Margaret Weston, who is no relation to Edith Weston either in family or politics. Mrs Edith Weston had been Chairman of the Library and Museum Committee since the library was opened. Her election as mayor was fully supported by Mr Willis as he made clear when, the next year, he seconded the vote of thanks to her as retiring mayor. The speech he made, as reported in the paper, tells us almost as much about Mr Willis as it does about Mrs Weston.

Mr Willis said he had been particularly fortunate in his relations with ladies in public life. When he was Mayor it was his great privilege to welcome to the Council the first lady Councillor, and as Chairman of the Bench it was his privilege to welcome the first lady magistrate of the Borough. A year ago, when the proposal was made that Mrs Weston should be elected Mayor, there was in certain quarters an element of apprehension, but that apprehension could now be seen as extraordinarily ridiculous. They had reason to regard Mrs Weston's service during the past year as an emphatic vindication of the action they took a year ago. The meetings of the Council had followed their customary order because they were

*under the control of a competent chairman. Mrs Weston had taken
an eager and consistent interest in the responsible work of the
Bench, and if the penalties that had fallen on unfortunate
delinquents had not been pronounced in thunderous tones they
might have seemed lighter because they were uttered gently.*

*If ever there was a year when convention would have called
for a man's head at the head of affairs, this had been such a year.
Yet they chose a woman, and they had no reason to regret their
choice. Mrs Weston threw herself with the utmost self-sacrifice into
the desperate work that went on behind the scenes in the recent
crisis. Whether it was that the Irish blood in her veins made the
atmosphere of conflict agreeable to her he did not know, but they
knew that Mrs Weston did enjoy the clash of ideals and that she
could stand up to a buffeting without loss of dignity or temper; and
today they paid tribute to one who had successfully faced tasks that
would have taxed a man's resources, and through them all had
retained the charm of her womanhood.*

The 'recent crisis' referred to was the Munich Crisis when Britain was on
the brink of war and Prime Minister Neville Chamberlain flew back
from his meeting with Herr Hitler in Munich, waving a piece of paper,
saying 'It is peace in our time.' Less than a year later, World War 2 had
started. After the 'phoney war' of the winter of 1939, came the
'blitzkreig', ending with the evacuation of Dunkirk.

My memories of the summer of 1940 are of days of endless sunshine
with the smoke trails of fighter aircraft forming patterns in the blue sky
above. As we lived near Chichester where I was in my last term at
school, and Tangmere airfield was only three miles the other side of the
city, I saw quite a bit of the Battle of Britain. The quiet market town of
Basingstoke, population 15 000, and 40 miles from the coast, didn't see
much enemy activity; that is until Friday 16 August.

That Friday morning Mr Willis left his home, 37 Burgess Road,
walking down Vyne Road as usual to work. In the afternoon his
housekeeper went shopping and then called on her mother who had
previously worked for Mr Willis and was then living at Page's
Almshouses. Next door, at number 35, Mr Rope had gone to work,
intending to stay late, because his wife and their son Philip had been
invited by the Musselwhites to join them for a picnic in the countryside.
Along the road at number 41, Mr and Mrs White stayed at home. Their
daughter, with her husband and their seven-year-old daughter, always
came to tea on Friday.

At ten minutes past five, either six or twelve bombers – accounts differ – appeared crossing Basingstoke from the south. One stick of bombs was dropped to the south of the railway line, and another in the Southview area on the north side of the station. When the Rope family got home they found that both 35 and 37 had been badly damaged. Their front door had been sucked out by the blast. At number 37 a tree had crashed into the kitchen where Mr Willis's housekeeper might well have been working. Number 41 had received a direct hit. The Whites and the Dicksons were in the garden having their tea. They were all killed except for Mrs White.

Mr Willis's housekeeper was still with her mother when Mr Willis came to tell her the news. They spent the night at his sister's house. Everyone in the Burgess Road area was evacuated. During the night an unexploded bomb went off which completed the demolition of numbers 35 and 37. Several people who had been looking at the damage in the evening had been standing on the spot where the bomb was buried.

The first bombs which were dropped fell around the parish church, destroying old houses around Church Square, damaging the Methodist Church so badly that it was later demolished and smashing the windows in St Michael's Church. This bombing was a double blow to Mr Willis. Shock waves from the bombs also smashed the windows of the museum, which was some distance away. One family living over their shop two doors away from the museum went back again after the windows were repaired and reglazed but the museum was closed and did not open again for three years.

Chapter Six

1940–1954 Freeman of Basingstoke

'It was a most happy and wonderful time on Thursday, wasn't it?'

After staying with his sister for six weeks, Mr Willis had the opportunity of renting a house in Eastrop Lane. He lived there for several years until the owner wanted it back, and then he moved to another house in Fairfields Road where he stayed until the end of the war. In both cases it was friends who offered him the use of their home. At Christmas 1940 Mr Willis's housekeeper Nora was visited by her friend Tom Goddard who had come home on seven days embarkation leave. The couple decided to get married before he went abroad. With the help of the pastor of the Congregational Church the licence was obtained and they were married on Boxing Day. Mr Willis was a witness at their wedding. The next day Nora saw her husband on to the train at Reading. It was four years before he came back, after service in North Africa and the Middle East.

Mr Willis's youngest sister Dorothy had returned to England at the outbreak of the war, having spent many of the previous years in South Africa. She was working in London but always came back to Basingstoke at the weekends to stay with her brother. On Saturday evenings she usually joined her sister Nellie and her husband at their home, but George was more likely to stay at home working or reading. At Christmas they all gathered at the Jukes' house.

The Basingstoke Museum reopened in November 1943. Mr Edwin Jewell, who had just retired, was appointed as warden, a position he held until his death. Mr Willis found that 'his friendly personality was a distinct asset to the museum both in the welcoming of strangers and in the encouragement and control of children.' Mr Jewell was the oldest of the lay preachers connected with the Congregational Church. He was another of the many friends of Mr Willis, particularly among the business community, who worshipped at the Congregational Church.

Mr Jewell was not needed to control the children if Mr Willis was there to talk to them. In November 1949, the Commercial class from Fairfield's School was taken on a visit to the museum,

where Mr Willis kindly showed us round. Looking at the cases was like making a journey through history. He told us that about

8 000 000 years ago, Basingstoke was buried under the sea. We were then shown implements of the Stone Age, such as flints in the shape of knives, arrow heads, axes and swords. Mr Willis told us that Stone Age men worked very hard to make these tools, as that was all they had to protect themselves. Relics from the Bronze and Iron Ages included boiling pots and pans.

The Museum also includes some interesting exhibits such as beautiful tapestry, lace, coins and seals, a motor-cycle and a penny-farthing bicycle. Jewellery exhibited includes watches, bracelets and lockets with photographs with hair in them, all of historical value.

We spent a most enjoyable afternoon and I think everybody would like to thank Mr Willis.

Several young people were encouraged by these visits to develop their own studies of local history. Robert Brown, who went with Fairfield's School to the museum around this time, has made the largest collections of anyone of photographs of Basingstoke, recording its changes, and has published several books of photographs with notes of relevant history. John Pearce, who used to call in at the museum of an evening in the hope of finding Mr Willis there and talking to him, took up the study of local transport and is co-author of a book on the Venture bus company. The artist Diana Stanley, having moved here from London, was inspired by her visits to the museum to record the old town in paintings which were reproduced with her account of the town's history in her book *Within Living Memory*.

It was not only at the museum that Mr Willis was encouraging young people to take an interest in the town and the local countryside. Hilda Wood, the headmistress of the Girls' High School, remembers

... many a budding young naturalist or archaeologist being seen in Mr Willis's shop showing him over the counter a flint or a flower for which he or she was shyly seeking identification. They would bend over it together in shared absorption

The museum had ceased to be the property of Basingstoke, having been transferred, in 1945, as a place of further education, to the County Council under the terms of the Education Act of 1944. Mr Willis continued to serve as the honorary curator.

Two years later an exhibition which Mr Willis helped to arrange attracted the attention of *The Times* special correspondent. Under the headline 'Archives displayed – An English Town down the Centuries', he wrote,

At Basingstoke Town Hall on Wednesday the Duke of Wellington opened – unfortunately for one day only – a remarkably rich and varied loan collection of archives relating to the town and its neighbourhood. It was arranged in connexion with the National Register of Archives, and was the first exhibition of its kind to draw its material from so limited an area. The exhibits varied widely both in kind and date. The earliest, lent by the Duke of Wellington, came from the Roman town of Silchester, and included a fine bronze eagle, perhaps the only surviving standard of a Roman Legion.

The Duke also lent documents illustrating the life of the first duke as a country gentleman. Other documents told the story of the parish of South Warnborough, from the Court Rolls of the reign of Richard II to the ARP papers of World War 2, and there was a collection of documents from The Vyne, the great country house, just to the north of Basingstoke, which is now a National Trust property.

The Roman eagle which, of course, was not a document, had special significance for Mr Willis. The first time he saw it, I am told, was at the Duke's home Stratfield Saye. Mr Willis had made one of his regular visits to overhaul the clocks. The Duke, talking to him afterwards, asked him whether he had any particular ambition. 'To hold the Roman eagle in my hands,' was Mr Willis's immediate reply. The Duke did not comment, but after leaving the room, came back a few minutes later with the eagle which he handed to Mr Willis. I have also been told that in later years he was able to borrow it to show at the annual dinners of Queen Mary's Old Boys. Almost nothing is known about the eagle, which is without wings and has nothing to identify the Legion, for which it was their most sacred emblem. The novelist Rosemary Sutcliff ascribed it to the Ninth Legion and wrote an enthralling historical novel, *The Eagle of the Ninth*, to explain how it came to be at Silchester.

It was in May 1945, during the last months of the war, that Mr Willis was elected a Fellow of the Society of Antiquaries of London. His name had been proposed by Mr O.S.G. Crawford and by another eminent archaeologist, Mr C. Hawkes. Both men were fellow members of the Hampshire Field Club. It was an honour he richly deserved but one he very nearly missed. When a ballot was held for the election of candidates Mr Willis received 20 'yes' votes and 5 'no' votes. One more vote against him and he would have failed to be elected. There are three possible reasons for this. He was described as a 'Jeweller and Optician' and the Society was prejudiced at that time against admitting people who were 'in trade'. Another similar reason was that Mr Willis had not had a university education, and lastly Mr Crawford was critical of the Society and, in his usual manner, had made his feelings known. I am fairly sure Mr Willis never knew that the vote nearly went against him.

After the war Mr Willis decided to buy a house in Bounty Road, not far from Fairfields School which he had attended as a boy. Before buying it he asked his housekeeper and her husband if they were happy about moving there. When Tom Goddard had returned from the war Nora had offered to resign, thinking he would not want to share his house with a married couple, but he had urged them to stay on. Later, when she was expecting a baby, she again offered to leave but once more Mr Willis asked her to stay. He felt he would get used to having a baby around. He didn't like changes in his domestic life, having to get used to new people in the house. His loyalty to the few people who worked for him was repaid by their loyalty. He never, Nora has said, complained.

Looking after Mr Willis was not, however, an easy job. He still took only a week's holiday each year, going down to the West Country by car now, for a walking holiday. He came home most days for a midday meal, and then came back again late in the evening for supper, having been to the museum or to a meeting. Thursday afternoons and Sundays were still spent walking. Horace Carey, who had been in business in Church Street since 1924, took the place of John Ellaway when the latter had to give up due to ill health. On Sundays they would go off with a flask and sandwiches. Sometimes a group of friends would go. When he came back he would come in with muddy boots, taking his handkerchief out of his pocket, having used it to wrap flints to carry them home. Number 44, Bounty Road, which was to be his home for the rest of his life, had the advantage of being nearer to the shop than Burgess Road.

Finding wild flowers was still as important as finding flints. In June 1948 he and Mr Burrows organised a botanical ramble to some of the more out-of-the-way spots of north-east Hampshire for over 40 members of the Hampshire Field Club. The party met at Micheldever in the morning and, travelling by coach, went on to Ibworth, Silchester and Sherborne where tea was taken. They came back with a large collection of wild flowers.

The threat of extinction to the rarer plants by new methods of farming and the loss of habitats was still in the future. Mr Willis is credited with discovering some new varieties. One of these is the Large Venus's Looking-glass, *Legousia speculum-veneris*, which he found sometime during the war years in a cornfield near Wooton St Lawrence. This is recorded in a recent publication, *The Flora of Hampshire*, by Lady Anne Brewis. Mr E.A. Burrows, who was Mr Willis's colleague in organising the botanical ramble, was a Basingstoke solicitor who, with his wife, wrote books on the local flora. They also specialised in keeping chows – dogs which gave Mr Willis a noisy welcome when he called at the house.

During these two decades the museum was building up a collection of clocks and watches which was recognised as one of the best in the country. The earliest clocks and watches to be donated were, I assume, given by Mr Willis. Sometimes when a client of his had died the relatives would give him any timepieces they found when clearing out the house. There is no doubt he bought anything of interest he saw in house sales or sales of antiques. The most famous item of this kind in the museum was the sixteenth-century German 'Stackfreed' clock-watch with its peculiar mechanism used as one of the earliest attempts to equalise the pull of the mainspring between its wound-up and run-down periods. In an article in the September 1952 edition of *The Clock & Watch Collector*, the writer says that the chances of the average enthusiast of acquiring one of these is extremely remote.

It is less than twenty years ago, however, that a very fine example came under the hammer among a small collection of other antiques at a country house sale near Basingstoke, and was bought for the local museum by Alderman G.W. Willis, JP, its active founder who still finds time to carry on his old established watch and clock-maker's business in the town. He cheerfully admits to having acquired the watch for the slightly fantastic sum of two pounds.

The museum's collection first began to take shape as a pocket history of several centuries of watchmaking when a Mrs A.S. Bates gave the museum a collection of seventeenth- and eighteenth-century watch cases. Other examples of watch-making were given by local people and the other firms in the town. There were watches actually made in the town by the Gregorys, whose shop was almost next door to the premises used by Mr Willis's grandfather.

There were also tools given by the Lodders, the firm that had trained his father. By 1960, if not before, the museum's collection of clocks and watches was recognised beyond Basingstoke. A paper published by the Antiquarian Horological Society in 1974 listed fifty-two museums in the United Kingdom, outside of London, with horological collections; of these the Willis Museum was one of twelve museums whose collections were marked as 'very important'.

Writing to his sister Edith, in the summer of 1960, Mr Willis wrote,

On Sat. I am expecting a visit at the Museum of the Antiquarian Horological Society led by Dr Ward of the Science Museum to see our Clock collection. As this is Saturday afternoon I shall be 'out of business' for the only Saturday afternoon I have ever been (except for holidays) & illness but it is something of an honour to be recognised by these high level experts.

An account of this visit was written by the Society's librarian. The Society members were impressed by the large collection of clocks, watches and allied tools which Mr Willis had built up over a long period, many of which they were free to handle and which they hoped they replaced over their correct labels. The star exhibit was still the 'Basingstoke Stackfreed' watch which one expert considered to be the best-preserved example of its type in the country. This and another valuable carriage clock were, unfortunately, stolen from the museum a few years ago. After the visit the party took tea at the Station Hotel.

More than twelve years earlier John Ellaway, Mr Willis's constant companion for so many years, had retired as librarian and assistant curator because of ill health. Early the next year, in 1948, the mayor, together with Alderman E.A. Weston and Alderman G.W. Willis called on him at his home to present him with an illuminated address in recognition of his service to the town. When Mr Ellaway died in 1950, Mr Willis referred, in the obituary he wrote for the *Hants & Berks Gazette*, to the friendly rivalry between him, Mr Ellaway and Mr Rainbow in accumulating their individual collections of fossils and flints which later they all gave to found the museum.

Another area of research had been the hunt for scratch dials or Mass clocks – rough sundials incised on the south walls of churches, for the priest's use in timing his services. This had involved a visit to every parish church in the district. Another very important contribution Mr Ellaway made to the knowledge of local history was the series of talks, called 'Itineraries', he gave to the Rotary Club, which were printed in the *Hants & Berks Gazette*. These were given over a period from 1936 to 1940, and described the historical and archaeological associations, attaching to the main roads leading out of the town. Mr Willis said his friend was naturally of a retiring disposition and would only commit himself to print under the pressure of personal persuasion. There is little doubt as to who applied the pressure. The time was coming when Mr Willis would receive the recognition which he was always concerned others should get.

The news that Mr Willis was to be made a Freeman of Basingstoke first appeared in the *Hants & Berks Gazette* on 26 March 1954.

> *The Council met in the Haymarket Theatre, originally built as the Corn Exchange, on 8 April to confer upon Alderman G.W. Willis the Freedom of Basingstoke, in recognition of his many and lifelong services to the town. The resolution was moved by Alderman W.H. Musselwhite who recounted Mr Willis's activities since he was first co-opted to the Council in 1916 – his outstanding year as Mayor, his last twenty-one years of unbroken and extremely valuable service as Councillor and Alderman, serving for much of that time as Chairman of the Water Supply Committee and of the Estates Committee. He went on to remind the Council of the other contributions Mr Willis had made to his native town – the creation of the museum, which the speaker hoped would, one day, be known as the Willis Museum, his involvement with the town's ancient charities, his service on the governing boards of Queen Mary's School and the Girls' High School, and as borough and county magistrate.*
>
> *Concluding, Alderman Musselwhite said, 'To all these activities and many more that I have been unable to mention, he has brought an acute and observant mind, a desire to see both sides of every question, an ability to express himself clearly and concisely, and a quiet and modest manner that has endeared him to every one of us. In all the years that I have known him I have never known him say an unkind or thoughtless word: throughout his life he has borne malice or ill will to none, and he has kept ever before him the ideal of service to his day and generation.'*

The motion was seconded by Councillor Russell Howard who, a few years later, would also be honoured by being made a Freeman. He was followed by Councillor Mrs Weston and Councillor Rigby Dale. Mrs Weston recalled the years during which she had worked closely with Mr Willis as chairman of the Library and Museum Committee and went on to recount anecdotes of those days. Most unfortunately none of these anecdotes was reported.

Colonel Rigby Dale was senior partner of the firm of Simmons & Sons, estate agents, who still operate from the same building next door to the Haymarket Theatre. He said, '... professionally he was a person who thought he knew a little bit about real estate. What had struck him so very much was the great technical knowledge Alderman Willis had displayed with regard to very difficult technical questions relating to the Council's considerable landed estates. It showed he had studied for many years to give advice and service as chairman of that committee.' This was the Estates Committee, of which Mr Willis was chairman. Colonel Rigby Dale was chairman of the Finance and General Purposes Committee. He said, 'if you ever had the misfortune to be chairman of a committee you will know that when difficult matters crop up, there are certain places you look around to naturally, because you know that if you look at those people you will get good, sound advice.' Whenever difficult matters had arisen in the Finance and General Purposes Committee he had been able to look to the left-hand corner where Alderman Willis customarily sat.

None of the speakers at the Freedom ceremony is still alive, but a friend of ours who was a junior planning officer in the years just before Mr Willis left the council remembers that Mr Willis rarely spoke at meetings but when he did everybody listened with great interest. They knew he would have something worthwhile to say.

The Mayor put the motion to the Council and it was carried unanimously. The Town Clerk read the illuminated scroll, and the Mayor presented the scroll and the hardwood casket, in which it is still kept in the Mayor's office, to Alderman Willis. 'When Alderman Willis turned from receiving the casket to reply he was greeted by a burst of spontaneous applause and was evidently much moved.'

In his reply he said, 'Mr Mayor, Ladies and Gentlemen – This is something I did not expect to say. I am trying to get back to a sense of reality. After all the compliments which have been paid to me today, I hardly recognise myself.

'Seriously this is the supreme moment of my life, and the realisation of that fact does not make it any more easy for me to express my deep appreciation and thanks for what you have done. The freedom of the borough is the greatest honour a civic community can confer on one of its citizens. I find it very difficult to reconcile what you have done with anything I have done or tried to do.' The honour was increased by the fact that in its long history Basingstoke had never made one of its citizens a Freeman before.

Explaining that it was excusable to reminisce, Mr Willis recalled the various events of his life and his personal feelings at these different stages, much of which I have already quoted. He was conscious of having outlived so many friends who had shared his activities. Now he was one of the very last overseers remaining; the last surviving member of the Town Council he later joined; none of the mayors who preceded him were still alive; and he was the last surviving founder member of the Rotary Club. His speech at the time is recorded.

> *I find myself something of a relic – in other words a 'fossil', and the discovery gives me a great deal less pleasure than other 'fossils' I have found ... To the council who have promoted this ceremony today and for this gift you are giving me ... to the very many, many friends from whom I have received congratulations and good wishes – an unexpectedly good number, to all of you who have honoured me with your support and presence today, may I say the good, old, time worn Anglo Saxon phrase, filled with all the sincerity and feeling I can put into it – thank you!*

Everybody then left the theatre, walked up Wote Street into the Market Place, entered the Town Hall, and walked up the stairs, past the carved stone bust of Colonel John May, to the room occupying the whole of the first floor, where the luncheon was being held. This may have been a double cube room. Around the room hung some six or seven large oil paintings which, in more recent times, the Council had valued. As they were worth more than the Council had thought, and appeared to have no relevance to Basingstoke, they were sold. Only the staircase remains. The bust of Colonel May was moved to the new civic offices. When developers took over the building from the Council in the early 80s, they added another floor inside this room. The Town Hall is now the Willis Museum.

Returning to 1954, a large number of people had accepted the invitation to the luncheon in the new Freeman's honour, including Sir Charles Chute, Bart. who was chairman of the County Council. When the mayor and Alderman Willis took their places at the head table they were warmly acclaimed. After an excellent four-course luncheon, the loyal toast was drunk, and then Sir Charles Chute proposed the toast 'The First Honorary Freeman of Basingstoke'. Alderman Willis, when he rose to reply, was greeted with very loud applause. He said,

> *I am conscious of a certain amount of incongruity in the function of today – you have honoured me for doing all the things I wanted to do and like doing. I have a craft which is interesting and satisfying, one in which head and hands combine and that is one of the activities which bring great satisfaction. I am happy in my job. As I*

said earlier, I have been to a good many committees and find pleasure in the sifting of ideas and their correlation towards a just decision, and then you say "Thank you" to me for it. I have liked serving on the Bench. There again there is this sifting of the evidence and trying to get to the kernel of the truth. Again you say 'Thank you'.

When speaking of his personal interests of archaeology, history and pre-history, he said he was 'conscious of saying this in the presence of one of the most distinguished of archaeologists – one who has done more than anyone else to put the science of archaeology on a firm basis in the past 20 or 30 years.' This was Mr O.G.S. Crawford. Mr.Willis went on to reminisce of his school days, of his countless expeditions in the countryside around Basingstoke where he said he became an inveterate trespasser, adding that his knowledge of public footpaths had been acquired so that he could escape if met by authority. Now all the local landowners welcomed him, but that took a little from the thrill of escape he had enjoyed in the past. He acknowledged his debt to Mr Allnutt whose contribution had made the creation of a museum possible, and to his colleagues who had worked with him in the museum. He spoke of the pleasure he had had in being a governor of Basingstoke's schools, and ended with the words 'Thank you'.

The Duke of Wellington had sent a telegram apologising for not being able to attend the ceremony. Among the letters of congratulation that Mr Willis received was one from Toronto, from his old school friend Sid Buckland (one of the few addressed to 'Dear George'), one from John R. Knowles who commented, 'you didn't say you were also a good leg puller', and another in the same vein from his nephew, Brian Jukes.

From the Vicar of Great Waltham, Essex
My most honoured, revered and famous uncle
Congratulations
Do tell us what it means to be a Freeman.
Does it mean you can go to the Cinema
every time you want without paying?
Brian.

Brian's son and daughter remember how their father and Uncle George used to tease each other. Before he was married Brian sometimes went with his uncle on walking holidays that were organised by the Holiday Friendship Club.

A few days after the Freeman ceremony Mr Willis received a letter from his sister Edith who had gone back to her home in north London. It clearly shows the admiration she had for her brother, admiration which present generations of the Willis family still have for 'Uncle George'.

April 11th 1954
Dear George
Honourable Freeman of Basingstoke!
(as well as Honorary)
It was a most happy and wonderful time on Thursday, wasn't it? I think you were really able to enjoy it too? weren't you? Any way you made excellent speeches, as well as the others who appeared to be really happy in their task.

It is very good to know you have enjoyed your work during such a large part of your life. Certainly it makes it twice the value to others also, if it is done and given with enthusiasm. I hope, if some avenues are closing down, others will open up. Are you going to write your memoirs & reminiscences some day? I thought when you were giving your speeches they were very suitable for the beginning of your book – which could then go on to include so much of interest & information to so many people, especially to your own town folk.

I do hope to visit the Museum again some day. It is good to know it is fulfilling such an educative purpose among the youth of Basingstoke.

Kon and Tiki are sitting at my feet as I write, in great contentment to have me home again and a fire!

It is nice to have the light days, but I hope it will get warmer soon.

Much love to you and my congratulations to add to those of the populace – for a well deserved honour!
Your Edith

How many writers, I wonder, have found the guidelines they should follow in a letter, written more than forty years earlier, and kept in the Hampshire Record Office at Winchester?

G 1920 *Willis's shop in Wote Street with Mr Willis in the doorway*

H 1928 *George Willis wearing his Rotary badge (51)*

I 1923 *George Willis as mayor (46)*

J 1933 *John Ellaway, Herbert Rainbow, George Willis (56) looking for flints*

K 1964 *George Willis in the Museum (86)*

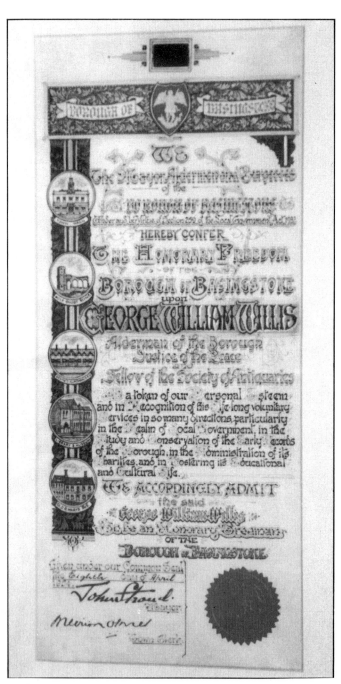

L *The scroll presented to George Willis when he was made a Freeman of Basingstoke*

Chapter Seven
1954–1960 The Last Independent

'I shall miss being at the centre of things.'

Towards the end of 1954, Mr Willis was offered another honour which he would have valued as much as being made Freeman. This was an honour he regretfully declined as he explained in his letter to the Duke of Wellington.

> *Your Grace*
>
> *I am very conscious of the honour of being invited to become President of the Hampshire Field Club – conveyed to me in such kindly terms. But my immediate reaction and subsequent consideration compel me to say that I do not feel able to accept this position.*
>
> *I am nearly 80 years of age and am only too well aware of rapidly increasing limitations in mind and memory, while my business commitments are as insistent and strenuous as ever they were. I am in process of relinquishing my former activities rather than of adding to them.*
>
> *It is with great regret that I feel unable to assist the Club in this way and I hope it may be possible to convey to the Council my sense of the honour they have shown me in this invitation which I regard as one of the highlights of my life.*
>
> *Sincerely*
> *G.W. Willis*

Two years later the Duke of Wellington and Mr Willis, together with the Bishop of Winchester, shared the same platform, as principal guests, when his old school – Queen Mary's – celebrated the 400th anniversary of the school's being granted its royal charter by Philip and Mary. The Duke unveiled a plaque; the Bishop preached a sermon; and Mr Willis gave an address in which he reviewed the history of the school over the last four hundred years. The notes which Mr Willis made in preparation for his talk still exist. They consist of odd pieces of paper, covered all over with writing, put into a small, brown envelope, every part of which is also covered with his notes. How he kept the thread of his talk in his mind I can't imagine. He was then nearly eighty.

In 1958 Mr Willis was the subject of a talk by John Arlott, giving him the ephemeral fame that is peculiar to radio and television. This was one of the few occasions when he received recognition at a national level. Apologising to his sister Edith, in a letter he wrote in March that year, he said:

Dear old Diff

I'm very sorry that you missed the broadcast as you would have been interested even though I say it who shouldn't. I am perhaps partly to blame altho not much for I should have missed it myself but for a wire from the BBC saying JA would be on at 6.54. This arrived just as I was quietly dozing after lunch between 2 and 3, when I had my eye on the clock as I was meeting Carey as usual for our customary ramble. The idea of a phone call did not cross my mind – but really I had no idea what was to be said & whether it was worth calling attention to – I admit that now I usually put off doing anything that isn't urgent. I so often say to myself – well it won't matter a great deal if I don't.

That at any rate was my fault. It was J. Arlott at his typical best. He mentioned my collar stud showing over my tie and my battered hat with the wind blown hair beneath it & that I should be blushing all over as I listened which I told him by letter was all true.

He mentioned that I was 80 and worked 5 & half days a week at mending watches & clocks – & the rest I frankly forget.

I have asked if I could have a copy of the script for the family archives but so far nothing has come along.

I have had a few comments. On my way home the same night some unknown man came up to me & shook hands vigorously with hearty congratulations. On the Friday after the broadcast I went out to N. Warnborough to see to a clock for an old lady who asked whether I was the man who was spoken about on the wireless. I've noticed a twinkle in one or two eyes whom I have passed in the street as though the owners were recalling some association.

We haven't heard anything of Doff but suppose she is getting on alright.

Love & good wishes

George

I have also tried to get a copy of the script but there is no record in the BBC archives. John Arlott's first draft, describing Mr Willis, is kept at the Hampshire Record Office, but I believe that the broadcast also referred to Mr Willis's views on the vast changes that would be taking place in Basingstoke over the next few years. It interesting that despite Mr

Willis's extreme modesty he did recognise that the events of his life were worth preserving, even if this was only for future generations of the family.

The reference to his sister Dorothy, who he called Doff, means, I think, that she had gone back to South Africa for her last visit. This letter is one of the few among the half dozen, preserved at the HRO, which he ended 'Love & good wishes' instead of 'Affectionately'. Although Mr Willis had a very close relationship with his sisters, he was still living in an age when it was not considered proper to express the affection he felt.

These letters give us a glimpse of Mr Willis away from his normal round of work, civic affairs and the museum. Sometime near Christmas he would visit his sister Edith in London, where they would be joined by Dorothy. Edith had a great love of the theatre and always took her great-niece to the Golders Green Hippodrome when Mary stayed with her. Mr Willis would sometimes suggest a show he and his sisters might visit but he was content to leave the choice to Edith.

> Will you being booking up something for the Saturday? How about Cinerama again – if it has changed. It was a very exciting experience which I remember more than most things as my memory and hearing are failing with the years. Cinerama was cinema 'in the round'.

In other letters he wrote,

> Whatever does your reference to 'shocking hospitality at Xmas' mean? I didn't notice any lack of anything! It was very pleasant and I don't see why we should not have another taste of it before you leave. If you ever find a show that you think would suit the three of us give us due notice and we will come.
>
> As years go by there is an indefinite reaction against breaking the weekly routine, even for a pleasurable jaunt like a visit to 42, but it always turns out to be more than worth while and adds its quota to life.

Edith was at this time about to move to another house in the same part of London. On a later occasion Mr Willis wrote, 'I believe I once saw the old Ben Hur – years ago – & certainly read the book but should be glad to see it in its new form – and the house.' It seems extraordinary that Mr Willis found the time to read popular novels.

In 1955 he accepted the invitation to be the first chairman of the Basingstoke and District Natural History Society. From 1950 onwards Mary and George Smith who lived at Up Nately, a village a few miles out of Basingstoke, had been having informal meetings with friends who shared their interest in natural history. These meetings were held at the *Rose Inn* which was close to May's brewery. Then it was decided in 1955 to turn these informal meetings into a formal society. Mr Willis was the only person considered for the position of chairman. Indoor meetings were held monthly, still in public houses, and Sunday afternoon walks were arranged. For three years, from 1959, meetings were held in a most unusual venue – a ladies' hairdressing salon, with some members sitting under the driers. Mr Willis usually led the walks, pointing out fossils and identifying wild flowers as he went along.

The Borough Council passed a resolution in July 1956 that the name of the museum should be changed to the Willis Museum. This proposal was accepted by the Hampshire County Council, which now owned the museum, and the proposal came into effect later in the year. This recognition of the part Mr Willis had played in bringing the museum into existence was long overdue His own situation at the museum, however, had changed. He was no longer curator and had been given the title of Honorary Director. The County had appointed Mr C.N. Gowing to be professional curator at both the Curtis Museum at Alton and the Basingstoke Museum in 1951. When, in 1960, he moved to Aylesbury, Margaret Macfarlane, who had joined him as assistant curator in 1957, was appointed to succeed him as curator of both museums.

The relationship between Mr Willis, the experienced gifted amateur, and these younger professionals, appointed by the County Council with full authority to run the museum, cannot have been easy. Inevitably, Mr Willis ceased to spend as much time in the museum as he had done in the past. Many people in the town probably still regarded Mr Willis as the curator. Newspaper reports from this period show that reporters would go to either Miss Macfarlane or Mr Willis for the story when new discoveries were found, as happened some years later when a Roman coffin with skeleton was found during road excavations in Basingstoke. When Miss Macfarlane took over she found that the museum had been the victim of its own success. After more than twenty years of collecting there was no room to display all the objects properly. Many of them had been put in store and Miss Macfarlane was anxious to get these out. 'Until things have been rearranged,' she told the press, 'this will not be possible. At the present moment we have hardly room to breathe.'

Mr Willis was reminded that he was getting older when the Girls' High School celebrated its fiftieth anniversary. He had turned thirty when it opened in 1908. Now he was over eighty.

The headmistress, Hilda Wood, wrote:

> On the fiftieth anniversary of the opening of the school we all crammed into the then small assembly hall to listen to Mr Willis and representative old girls and members of staff talk of the old days of the school. Miss Costello was headmistress when Mr Willis became chairman and, of course, he remembered the school's opening at Brook House in 1908 and its transference to Crossborough Hill in 1912. I remember with what pleasure he joined in the party that followed, when he shared in the ceremony of the cake with its fifty candles.

After 1936 Mr Willis never had to stand again for election to the Council by the people of Basingstoke. The following year he was elected as an Alderman, and then re-elected by his fellow councillors every six years. He remained an Independent. He respected his fellow councillors for their ability, and if they shared his integrity, vision and pride in Basingstoke. Their political views were of no interest to him.

Then in May 1960 the political balance of the Basingstoke Town Council shifted. Writing to his sister Edith, Mr Willis reported,

> We have had a civic upheaval here at election time – the Cons. have swept back – 12 to 6 Lab. and are proceeding to run the Council. I understand the present 4 Aldermen, including me, will be re-elected next Thur. with another 6 years work ahead if I care to stay so long.

That Thursday was, however, to be his last day on the Council. As he explained in his next letter,

> The situation seems to have arisen from the failure of one councillor to sign the ballot paper he put in! The 6 Labour people all voted for 2 Lab. men only. The 12 Cons. had apparently arranged – 6 to vote for the 3 members to sit for 6 years & 6 to vote for 3 members to sit for 3 years which, of course, included me as the old man. Unfortunately one member spoilt his paper as above so I only got 5. They had carefully arranged for a Cons. member to take the chair & so have a casting vote but as 2 Lab. men got their 6 votes he had to choose one of them.

After the result had been announced Mr Willis took off his new robe and handed it to Mr Howard. He smiled and told the grim-faced Council, 'It is a great relief and pleasure for me to retire in favour of Mr Howard. There is a certain element of relief for I am getting an old man.' He watched the proceedings for a short time and left quietly before the meeting closed. Later a friend phoned Mr Willis to congratulate him on his re-election, unaware that he had lost his place on the Council. The chairman of the meeting was John Peat. Margaret and I knew John. He was a man of great sincerity who worked tirelessly for Basingstoke, and whose career was cut short when he died of a heart attack while on a business flight to west Africa. Having to choose between Russell Howard and George Willis, both outstanding councillors, must have been a choice he wished he could avoid. Russell Howard, a trade union organiser and one of the first of the Labour men on the Council, also gave distinguished service to the town, and had been made Basingstoke's second Freeman in 1958.

As always Mr Willis accepted a change in his fortunes with equanimity. Quoting again from letters to his sister,

> I have no doubt all this party business will fade out when the Council gets to work. It is possible I shall miss being at the centre of things but I still have plenty to do & keep my mind alive – in fact I'm better than usual!' Some time later he wrote, 'I think I am beginning to appreciate leaving the Council, especially these light evenings when I can now sometimes get abroad and go flower hunting. It is a little curious to be 'out of things'.

Chapter Eight
1964 – The Mr Willis we knew

'I am a modest man and feel a little uncomfortable when I am over emphasised, as I sometimes am.'

I came to be involved with the Workers Educational Association and then with Mr Willis in an unusual way. Soon after moving to Basingstoke in 1962, I was sitting in a train at Waterloo, waiting for it to leave for Basingstoke, when the man sitting opposite me leaned forward and asked if I was interested in sociology. Not knowing how to answer that question, I ended up going to a public meeting a few evenings later to hear a talk given by Maurice Broady, Professor of Sociology at Southampton University, on the problems the town faced with the proposed expansion to take overspill from London. That meeting led to me joining a WEA study group on the subject, with Maurice as our tutor, which met weekly at the home of Basingstoke's probation officer. By the time that study group was wound up I was a committed WEA member. I moved on to join a local history study group which Margaret and I hosted.

Before that happened I had helped organise a five-day study tour of new towns and new buildings. As the only architect in the group I arranged meetings with town planners and architects while Maurice Broady fixed up for us to meet the social workers dealing with the problems created by new town development. The long weekend was a great success. We stayed in student accommodation in London and went out each day – visiting Basildon, Crawley, Harlow, Stevenage, the LCC housing at Roehampton and a variety of other modern building types. Maurice and I wrote a report which was published in the *Hants & Berks Gazette*. We then went on to consider holding a public meeting, showing the colour transparencies I had taken. I think it was Maurice who had the idea of recording the newspaper article on tape and playing it back while the slides were being projected. This was in the days when tape recorders were like large suitcases, only twice as heavy, and tape was wound on to spools seven inches (17.5 cm) or more in diameter. And that is how the first audio visual was invented. It was some time before I found out that I was not alone in making these.

Mr Willis wasn't, as far as I can remember, a member of the history group but he must have come to some meetings. One of our earliest memories of him is when we noticed an old car pull up in the road and saw him, a slim, small man wearing a battered trilby hat, and carrying an enormous leather-bound book, coming up the path. This was the document containing the records of the enclosure of the common fields which he had shown Stephen Usherwood more than thirty years earlier. I don't imagine Mr Willis asked if we wanted to see it. We were carried along by his own enthusiasm as he explained it and pointed out particular items that interested him. After a short time he left again. His car shot off to the end of the road, turning into Vyne Road with hardly time to check whether there was any other traffic about. It was hard to believe this new friend of ours was 85 years old.

One day I was looking at the syllabus, prepared by the WEA chairman Eric Stokes for the local history group, when I realised that it could be presented as an audio visual. The course covered the history of Basingstoke from earliest times to the present day. It was still possible to illustrate the history of the last few centuries with photographs of existing buildings, because development of the town had been frozen while arguments on how Basingstoke should be expanded were sorted out. Eric Stokes gave me his full support. One of the group members lent me her copy of Baigent and Millard's *History of Basingstoke*, the vicar lent me churchwarden's accounts, which in those days were kept in an old suitcase in the vicarage, and I set to work. At the weekends I walked around the town with my camera, and in the evenings, after getting home from the office in London, I scribbled away, expanding Eric's framework with quotations ranging from the grant of a royal charter to the town to the letters of Jane Austen. I was encouraged by the thought that there would be no mistakes in my script. I would be asking Mr Willis to read it. He would spot any errors.

My father was staying with us in July 1964 when I asked Mr Willis to come round one evening to see some of the photographs I had taken. One of my partners, Rupert Byerley, was also there. As I projected the slides Mr Willis was reminded of incidents in his long life. That was the first time I heard of the dancing bear, and how he saw Queen Victoria in her train at Basingstoke station. This needed to be recorded and I brought a tape recorder and a microphone into the room. Mr Willis was silenced but after a time he forgot the presence of the microphone and the conversation started again.

The picture on the screen at that moment was of a seed drill, looking much like a wheelbarrow. My father was explaining how it worked. He had used them when working on farms as a young man.

Mr Willis (GW)	Oh, that's a museum piece.
Derek Wren (DW)	I saw another one recently in the vicarage gardens.
GW	Then the museum had better appropriate it.
Harry Wren (HW)	I shouldn't think so. Fifty years ago you could see scores of them.
GW	Oh yes, well fifty years is the sort of thing the museum jumps at, because in fifty years time it will be a mystery.

Another slide was of the *Barge Inn*, then at the lowest end of Wote Street. This reminded Mr Willis of bargees sitting along the front of the inn, as barges came in to the wharf at the head of the canal on the other side of the road. The canal had ceased to be used and the area facing the *Barge Inn* turned into a timber yard when Mr Willis was a young man. Mr Willis then told us how the river Loddon had been diverted when the canal was built in 1794.

GW	The river ran round then, where now a row of shops has been built, and there was a very fine row of chestnut trees, made a beautiful entrance to the town, after the rather dreary Station Hill, coming from the station. I took a committee from the town council down, before the cinema was built, to suggest there should be a public park there, with trees and water gardens, but there were two very dreary councillors at the time, could see nothing beyond their own noses, I suppose, so the scheme was turned down.

Eastrop Park was built, just as Mr Willis had envisaged, but not in his lifetime. I could not have seen, that evening, that some six years later I would have the same reaction from a council committee that Mr Willis had experienced.

A slide showing the London Street Congregational Church, at the side of which is a narrow road called May Place, brought forth a surprising reaction from Mr Willis.

DW	The thing that rather intrigues me about the Congregational Church is its association with the May family.
GW	The May family?
DW	Weren't they largely connected with this?

GW	The brewery Mays?
DW	Well, that's what I was thinking
GW	Oh, I don't think so. I never heard the remotest connection. No, what I know about the Mays ...
DW	What about May Place Hall, then?
GW	Oh, I see. (*chuckle*) I think that was an Odiham May. Quite a different family to the brewery Mays. Oh, the brewery Mays – the Colonel May I remember would have been a super Anglican if anything – no connection with chapel.
	I remember him as a man who spent money freely in Basingstoke in order to obtain a knighthood, but he just evaded it.
DW	Is he the May who was mayor of the town?
GW	Yes, several times mayor – that is the man.
DW	That's interesting. It shows how easy it is to come unstuck in this field of local history.
GW	Perhaps it is well to get that straight (*we all laughed*) There is a book, by the way, published on the brewery May family. I don't know whether you have come across it. We have a copy, I think, in the museum. You can put yourself wise on the brewery Mays.

It is only recently that I have come across this book on the history of the May family, 'with particular reference to Colonel John May'. He and Mr Willis, both elected to the office of mayor, were as different as two people could be. John May, a colonel in the Hampshire Rifle Volunteers, not a regular soldier, rode around the town on his horse during the celebrations to mark Queen Victoria's Golden Jubilee. He lived in a large house he had built on the south side of the town. The colonel commemorated the Coronation of Edward VII by setting the lamp standard in the Market Place on a block of granite. The coronation was, however, only referred to on one side of the base. The other three faces were inscribed to show a likeness of the colonel himself and lists respectively of the years in which he had been mayor and the years in which other members of his family had held that position.

Mr Willis lived in a fairly small house, in a modest style and was always embarrassed at public notice. His income could never have allowed him to make a lavish display of his wealth, although in his own way, he was equally generous. John Arlott noted that:

... he was the first to put up the money to preserve the town's only timbered house from demolition and none of the old folk of the town who come to him for help go empty away.

The house referred to was probably some cottages, with jettied construction, just below the railway bridge in Chapel Street. Mr Willis gave £100 of the £150 required for their restoration. If this was the building it was one of the first to be demolished in the late 1960s. John Arlott was mistaken in thinking there were no other timbered buildings in the town.

Did Mr Willis's remarks reveal the other aspects of his character Geoffrey Civil had known? We shall never know. There was no bitterness in Mr Willis's comments – more an expression of quiet amusement. He was always forthright in his statements, although more tactful when speaking in public. Fortunately for the memory of John May, the Colonel is remembered in Basingstoke as a generous benefactor, which he was, also generous to his employees, sending them home at Christmas with a large turkey apiece.

The last slide I showed that evening was of St Michael's Church tower.

GW	Now that's the church tower, isn't it, and that white stone – at one time the church clock dial was at that point. We have got prints showing the clock dial where that white stone is – a most queer place.
Rupert Byerley	Would that be a type of bracket clock ?
GW	No, it was definitely in the turret. The present clock was given by Dr Sheppard, the last vicar by about six.

There was one photograph, at least, I still needed at that stage. This would be one of Mr Willis – in the museum – to illustrate the founding of the museum. Fortunately I was there one day when he was talking to the assistant curator and standing in front of a case displaying some of the clocks and watches. My camera was in my hand. I lifted it and took the photograph shown on the front cover. It shows Mr Willis as John Arlott remembered him, when he saw him at the back of the shop.

In his back room, once your eyes were accustomed to its filtered light, you could distinguish George from his assistant by flickers of reflected light. It winked back from the edges of his spectacles, the age-worn head of the collar stud which always showed above the knot of his tie and, least obtrusive but most revealingly, there was a gentle humorous twinkle in his eyes.

I was already in touch with John Arlott when Mr Willis spent that evening at our home. John had agreed to record my account of the history of Basingstoke, provided he could find time to do it when the cricket season ended, and on condition that my script contained no statement with which he disagreed. It was near the end of October before he was free from commentating. He came to our home in Basingstoke for the afternoon, where we had pulled the curtains in the back bedroom and draped blankets over them, for sound insulation, creating the most primitive studio which I suppose John Arlott ever used. It was also, he told us afterwards, the longest recording, without a break, he had ever made. Smoking a cheroot while he spoke, his voice became ever huskier as he went through the script from prehistoric times to town expansion. We were very fortunate that John Arlott gave us his time to make this recording. At the end of that year he suffered the first of the personal tragedies which saddened his last years when his eldest son was killed in an accident.

Another WEA member, Robert Monk, a research chemist and music lover, was in charge of the sound recording and had already recorded the other voices, such as my wife reading one of Jane Austen's letters. Now Robert had little more than a fortnight to cut and stitch the tape together before the WEA showed 'Basingstoke – The History of our Town'. Somehow it was done. I had made a few posters which we had put up around the town, and the *Hants & Berks Gazette* had given us some publicity. The WEA had booked the hall at Queen Mary's School, one of the largest in the town, but we had no idea what numbers to expect. We were, therefore, amazed when on Wednesday evening, 11 November 1964, as we went along to the school to set up the equipment, we saw people, coming from all directions, walking towards the school. When we were ready to start there were even people standing at the back. It was a nail-biting experience. Would those of us who had worked on the project be lynched if the audience were bored? There was silence for some time, then when the commentary reached the first of the humorous comments which I had managed to incorporate, there was laughter. We knew we had the audience on our side. When it finally ended there was silence again. It was probably for only a few seconds but seemed much longer, then everyone in the hall started applauding. John Arlott's contribution had worked the magic spell.

Percy Pitman, the regional secretary of the WEA, jumped on to the stage and called for me to join him. I was too shattered even to consider accepting his invitation. Then he called for Mr Willis. Again there was no movement. Mr Pitman paid us some very kind compliments, the audience left, we packed up the equipment and went home. A day or two later I received a letter from Mr Pitman, short but full of praise, and then a letter from Mr Willis.

Dear Mr Wren

May I offer my cordial congratulations on the unique success of your meeting – for it was so largely your doing that you cannot refuse most of the credit. I was frankly astonished and delighted – as it is so many years since I can recall a meeting of cultural and educational importance being held in the town. In my youth I welcomed occasional lectures – Gilchrist Trust etc. on popular science and natural history subjects but they died out with the spread of popular scientific literature and, of course, of wireless and TV. I was a little apprehensive, in fact, about an audience and now kick myself enthusiastically in view of the facts.

The whole arrangement was admirable, sections and music, while the photos were ideal. If I have a criticism it is in regard to the emphasis ? placed on myself. I very warmly appreciate the compliment of having been shown in connection with the museum – but feel I was shown too long! Even the Mayor only had a brief glimpse while I was under review during the whole time the museum report was read. I am a modest man and feel a little uncomfortable when I am over emphasised as I sometimes am.

Anyway I do appreciate your kindly treatment of what I did and I rejoice with you at the successful outcome of the immense amount of work which you put into the project.

You gave a pleasant and profitable evening to Basingstoke and me,

Sincerely yours,

G.W. Willis

We didn't see very much of Mr Willis in his later years. Work took up more and more of my time. I attended a course of WEA lectures on the history of Hampshire. Mr Willis was also a member of the class, and the only member who knew – I am sure – as much as the lecturer who was Mrs Barbara Carpenter-Turner, an outstanding historian. Mr Willis used to come quietly into the classroom and find himself a seat at the back of the room. He never spoke unless Mrs Carpenter-Turner asked him to corroborate or add to something she had told us.

On another occasion my wife and I, with our young family, joined a WEA outing to Ladle Hill which Mr Willis led.

One more memory remains when he was at our house and my wife brought him a cup of tea on a tray. 'Look the other way, please?' he said, with a smile, while taking four spoonfuls of sugar. He was interested on that occasion in our boys running around him, and said that family life was unfamiliar to him.

His great niece, Mary Dore, has told me that when she stayed with her grandmother in Basingstoke they rarely visited him at his home but called on him at the shop. She remembers the warm welcome Uncle George gave her and how they would stand in the workroom at the back of the shop talking. All around were clocks ticking, the sound being interrupted from time to time when one of the clocks chimed.

Chapter Nine
1960–1970 The Last Years

'I have the sense of being a stranger in a strange place.'

When my wife and I first met Mr Willis in 1964, four years had passed since his career as a councillor had abruptly ended. On 30 June 1960 the Borough Council had passed a resolution:

> *that this Council places on record its appreciation of the service given to the Council of the Borough of Basingstoke by GEORGE WILLIAM WILLIS ESQ., JP, FSA, Honorary Freeman of the Borough over a period of 37 years, and on behalf of the people of Basingstoke extends to Mr Willis its grateful thanks and best wishes for a happy retirement.*

Although he was 'out of things' as far as the work of the Council was concerned, Mr Willis had no thought then of giving up work. Writing to his sister Edith, some time in 1960, he said,

> *I am I suppose as well as I shall ever be (which I am glad to be able to say). I can't hear as well as once – nor sleep as well – but I am glad that I can still work & can at times get the satisfaction of doing difficult jobs satisfactorily.*

In another letter he wrote,

> *At the moment business – sales – are very slow and the work is overwhelming. We have been a collection of invalids. Mrs Wood is going to hospital for treatment of a painful knee. I've had a touch of lumbago that involved walking with bent knees – even Stanley has had a few days off with a bad throat. Still we have survived.*
>
> *Alice, our very competent assistant, will be leaving Jan. as her husband finishes military service. We are interviewing a schoolgirl tomorrow as a possible successor, but it will be hard going for Mrs W. for a time.*

Mr Willis felt uncomfortable when the people he saw daily had to leave his service. They remained as loyal to him as he was to them. Mr Willis had recovered from his attack of lumbago when he wrote. Further on in the letter, he said,

Today I've had my morning walk – along country lanes in brilliant sunshine & inconceivably beautiful. It has been a dream summer – its a pity that age dulls one's appreciation somewhat. However I'm still going strong.

Presided at the GHS prize day for the last time as I have declared 'retirement'.
Affectionately
George

Although Mr Willis retired as chairman of the governors of the Girls' High School in 1960, after serving as chairman since 1924, he was still a member of the Governing Board at the time of his death. Towards the end of 1960 Mr Willis appears to have offered to resign from Rotary. The Club granted him honorary membership, telling him he was always welcome but under no obligation to make the minimum number of attendances in a year which Rotarians are required to make. The letter from the secretary was addressed to him as 'Uncle George', but only older members of the club, and older members of Queen Mary's Old Boys' Association called him 'Uncle George'. To younger members he was a respected, almost revered, figure.

In 1961 the Basingstoke and District Natural History Society made Mr Willis a life president. Two years later he gave the Society the talk on the Basingstoke of his youth which was fortunately recorded and from which I have extensively quoted in Chapter One. That year – 1963 – started with a heavy snowfall which lay on the ground for weeks. It was the last occasion that Basingstoke has had any appreciable amount of snow. The Society had organised a social evening, held in the Sunday school room at the Immanuel Church. The membership was now too large for meetings to be held in public houses. Mr Willis arrived after everyone else, having worked late at the shop, to find that the two sets of doors leading into the school room were both closed. He banged on the door but no one heard him. After a while he went home through the snow. A trivial story, you might say, but Mary Felgate who was secretary to the society, as well a close friend of his niece, still remembers the embarrassment they all felt that their president, 'dear Mr Willis', had been shut out from their celebrations. When Mr Willis replied to his sister's letter over his failure to be re-elected as alderman, he said,

I have no regrets – as the Council is faced with very difficult problems in the near future & I shall be saved considerable thought & worry about them.

This was something of an understatement. The problems Basingstoke faced arose from the County Council's decision that Basingstoke must be expanded to take overspill population from London. As early as 1944 the Greater London Plan, prepared by Professor Abercrombie, recommended the expansion of existing towns, which were within 40 to 50 miles from London, as well as the building of new towns. Basingstoke was named as one of the towns to be expanded. By the late 1950s the first group of new towns, encircling London, was established. The London County Council had looked at 70 more sites in the south of England to find other places where they could build more new towns. One of these was the village of Hook, less than six miles east of Basingstoke, with an existing station on the railway line to London. It was also on the A30, linking London to Southampton and the west of England. Water supplies were adequate and the land was only of moderate agricultural value. The architects and planners of the LCC prepared a plan for a new town, one of the first of the so-called 'linear' plans.

The enthusiasm of the London County Council for this project was not shared by the people of Hampshire. By 1961 Basingstoke had already agreed, with some reluctance, to provide homes and factories for a limited number of Londoners. The Hook proposal ignored the fact that a line of towns already existed, forming a continuous development running south from Reading through to Farnham. If Hook was developed it would link with this on the east side and with Basingstoke on the west, so that Basingstoke would be on the western edge of London.

The Hampshire County Council was totally opposed to the idea of a new town at Hook, but the London County Council had the backing of the Government. At the end of 1959, when members of the Hampshire County Council briefed counsel to oppose the Hook scheme they were advised there was little chance of success unless alternative proposals for housing Londoners elsewhere were put forward. In other words accept the expansion of Basingstoke and Andover. In this game where Basingstoke had most to win or lose the Borough Council was the weakest player. Mr Willis argued for moderation, for considering the arguments and coming to a logical and rational conclusion. He could see, no doubt, that this development was inevitable, and could also see there would be long-term gains for the town. Now he was out of the game and could not influence the Council's views. John Arlott, the romantic, with his unforgettable memories of the Basingstoke of his boyhood, never accepted the development. To him it was a scandalous desecration of the town he had once loved.

The wind of change was blowing in other areas, as Mr Willis wrote in a short article on the merger and consolidation of the twenty-eight charities that existed in Basingstoke and with the administration of which he had been involved for many years. Now a new body called the 'Basingstoke Charities' had been formed in 1962, able to use the income, produced by the money and property given by local benefactors over several centuries, in ways that corresponded more effectively to the needs of the twentieth century. One of the customs that ended was the weekly distribution of bread which was made in the porch of St Michael's Church on Sunday afternoons. This had gone on for 300 years. Mr Willis regretted these changes but recognised that it was necessary to adapt to changing needs. He became the chairman of the new body. I doubt whether any other name was ever considered. He only held the position for a short time before stepping down, having been chairman for 37 years altogether, but stayed on as a trustee.

The next year saw the disappearance of another piece of Basingstoke's history. The clock tower on the old Town Hall, given to the town by Colonel John May in 1887, was declared unsafe. Before it was taken down Mr Willis went up a ladder and removed the clock for the museum. Newspaper reports noted that he was 82 and had been only ten when he had helped his father install the clock. When the tower was taken down it was found to be so unstable that there was a danger that it might collapse and the staff of Lloyd's bank, on the other side of the road, had to be evacuated until the job had been completed.

On another occasion about this time Mr Willis was up a ladder winding the clock on the roof of the bandstand in the Memorial Park when he fell. Bystanders quickly picked him up and got him to the hospital but it was found that he was not hurt. His great-nephew and niece remember 'the family's surprise at him still doing these sort of jobs in his 80s'.

He was, however, finding it difficult to do some jobs. One friend of ours remembers him coming out to a village just north of Basingstoke, to take away a grandfather clock for overhaul, which he removed with a struggle, and then ringing up some weeks later to say that he was unable to do the job. Finally in 1964 Mr Willis sold the firm to L.T. Humphreys Ltd of Andover, but he arranged to stay on working for the new owners repairing watches. Stan Adams, who had worked with him for nearly 60 years, also came back to do part time work. The newspapers came out with the headline ' At 86 George can't bear to retire'. Mr Willis was quoted as saying that he couldn't bear waking in the morning to face a day with nothing to do.

By the time Mr Willis sold the business, the Borough Council had accepted that it could not prevent Basingstoke being changed from a quiet market town, serving the countryside around it, to a medium-size industrial town accommodating London overspill. A tripartite committee, known as the Basingstoke Town Development Joint Committee, was established, made up of four councillors from Basingstoke and three each from London and Hampshire, under the chairmanship of a councillor from the Basingstoke Borough Council. This set up the Basingstoke Development Group, with Robert Steel as Director and Allan McCulloch as Chief Architect/Planner, to carry out the proposed changes. In August 1962 the *Hants & Berks Gazette* produced a special edition on the New Town Map, with the dramatic headline:

Basingstoke: South's first new town of the motor car age. Shopping centre on a platform: separate routes for cars and pedestrians. The showpiece town of the south of England. That will be the Basingstoke of the 1980s. Over the next 15 years great alterations will be made in the town centre, thousands of new homes and dozens of new factories will be springing up on new estates as the town soars to a population of 75 000.

The shopping centre was not built on a platform. The multi-storey car parks were put above and not below the shops. All the other proposals were carried out in accordance with the master plan. Inevitably in cases of development on this scale there were casualties. A high proportion of the town's traders who had occupied the same premises for several generations decided not to relocate but to retire and either move away from Basingstoke or into the surrounding villages. Except for that part of the town centre now known as the top of the town, which included Mr Willis's shop, the museum and the Haymarket theatre, the rest of the shopping area was completely cleared. That clearance swept away several houses, including eight listed buildings – Brook House, once the home of the Girls' High School, the bow-fronted brewery manager's house and Queen Anne House facing Church Square which today preservation groups would fight tooth and nail to preserve.

Basingstoke had not been helped by Nikolaus Pevsner who, in his *Buildings of Hampshire* had written, 'At present, for its size, the town is singularly devoid of architectural pleasures.' He also said, 'If Basingstoke really receives the new centre designed by Llewelyn-Davies, Weeks & Partners with Ian Fraser & Associates, it will get something worth looking at.'

Phase One of the new shopping centre was opened in November 1968. Although it is a competent job, designed when shopping centres on the scale and size of Basingstoke's were a new type of project, few people, I believe, would agree with Pevsner's views. If the integration of the centre into the existing fabric of the old town was part of the brief, it was obviously given a low priority.

The first area to be cleared and redeveloped, with shops built around a new square, was called New Market Square. This area, always intended to be temporary, is now [at the time of writing] about to be redeveloped. The main demolition, involving an area of 18 acres, did not take place until the late summer of 1966. Mr Willis was clearly very conscious of the changes that were happening and were going to happen. In a talk he gave in 1963 to the Natural History Society, now renamed the Basingstoke Field Society, he spoke of his recollections of Basingstoke as it was when he was a youngster.

Basingstoke today has changed completely; tumbled over itself to expand. It seemed in my early days a very settled place, where you knew almost everyone you passed in the street. There wasn't the sense of being a stranger in a strange place that has developed recently.

Towards the end of 1965 another link with his youth was broken with the death of his sister Ellen. The funeral was held at the Congregational Church where she had worshipped since the time of her marriage. Her husband had died some years earlier. The list of mourners, published in the paper, included Kathleen Wornham, described as close friend and companion. She had been taken on by Ellen as a maid when she left school, and is now regarded by Ellen's grandchildren as a member of the family. Neither of Mr Willis's other two sisters were then living in Basingstoke. Edith was in London and Dorothy in Hove. I have been surprised that many people who knew Mr Willis much better than I did were unaware that he had these sisters.

When demolition of the town centre began on a large scale, hoardings went up around the buildings, leaving the roads still open for traffic and pedestrians. As you walked along the streets you could see the demolition workers ripping off roof tiles and tearing out windows. Then the bulldozers moved in to complete the job. Trucks moved in and out clearing the rubble. Everything that would burn was stacked on giant bonfires that burned for days. When the dust had cleared and the bonfires had burnt themselves out, the hoardings were taken down.

From the east end of St Michael's Church there was an uninterrupted view across open space to the gas holders in the distance. There was an eerie silence and 'no birds sang'. On the south side of this space the demolition included the Immanuel Church but the chemist's shop next door, with the home above where Mr Willis's sister and her husband had once lived, was spared. Mr Willis had reached an age when familiarity meant a great deal. Now even the church where his father had taught him in the Sunday school was gone.

He was, however, still active; in fact too active. At the age of 90 while driving his car – a Mini – he changed lanes on the A30, colliding with two other cars. He was prosecuted for dangerous driving but because he was still on the Supplemental List of Magistrates the case was heard at Odiham. After leaving the court, where he had been fined £15, he said, 'After this accident I am finished with driving.' It was typical of Mr Willis to cut out the newspaper reports and paste them in his scrapbook (which can be seen on microfilm in the Basingstoke library). A lesser man would have tried to cover up his mistake.

It may have been about this time, but we have no record to confirm the year, that when Margaret and I saw Mr Willis at a public meeting he told us of his failing faculties. Some people's minds remain active to the very end. Many people suffer from failing intelligence and loss of the senses without being aware that this is happening. Mr Willis was conscious of these failures and this grieved him. His last years were, sadly, years of difficulty. Mr and Mrs Goddard had moved out of 44, Bounty Road to their own house a few doors away. Mr Willis was never able to find housekeepers who cared for him as Nora Goddard had done. There was less now that he could contribute to the work of the museum. He continued, however, to keep his mind active. Mary Felgate began to type his articles which in the past he had always written by hand. He visited her for coffee in the evening to discuss his ideas, and then as he became more frail, she would walk back with him to Bounty Road.

Happily, there was no loss of respect for Mr Willis in his old age. On one occasion, when new roads were being built as part of Basingstoke's redevelopment, gold coins were unearthed. Because of the value of these a coroner's court was convened to decide whether they should be treated as 'treasure trove'. Mr Willis was a member of the jury. Barbara Applin, the assistant curator of the museum, was present. The coroner's first task was to appoint a foreman of the jury, who were standing in a line in front of him. Mr Willis was at one end of the line. When the jury was asked to recommend someone, one of them suggested a man who was at the other end of the line. 'An excellent suggestion,' said the coroner, looking instead directly at Mr Willis. So Mr Willis was foreman and the jury had the one person in Basingstoke who knew anything about the subject.

In July 1967 Mr Willis told a meeting of the Aldworth Foundation that he wished to resign as chairman. He regretted that, owing to his age, he no longer felt able to act in that capacity. His resignation was accepted in August of the following year, but he accepted the invitation to remain on the board. He had been chairman for 43 years, during which time he only missed one of the meetings of which two were held each year. The last meeting he attended was on 12 November 1969. He only had three months more to live.

A stroke made speech difficult. When his sisters came to visit him they would suggest the words he was struggling to say. This annoyed him. His great-niece's husband showed more understanding, and would sit with him patiently waiting for him to find the word he was seeking. There were times when his mental faculties would rally. Only a few months before his death he asked Miss Hunt, of the Girls' High School, to lend him her *Sixth Book of the Aeneid* so that he might read again of the hero's journey to the underworld. Hilda Wood, the school's headmistress, visited him in hospital when his memory of the present and of people had become rather dim. She mentioned the High School to identify herself. 'Ah,' he said, smiling, his eyes lighting up, 'you say the words and it all comes flooding back to me.'

Mr Willis was 92 when he died on 13 February, 1970. Russell Howard, who had been a close friend and who had served with him for many years on the Council, and who was the only other person at that time to have been made a Freeman of Basingstoke, died 36 hours later. The funerals of both men took place on successive days at the parish church of St Michael. Both funerals were civic occasions with the mayor, Dudley Keep, attending with other councillors. Among the flowers at Mr Willis's funeral was a wreath from John Arlott. One lady, whose family had had a happy relationship with both Mr Willis and his father, felt that when she attended the funeral the last link with the Basingstoke they all knew had been severed.

Many tributes were paid to Mr Willis. Horace Carey, who had been his companion for so many Thursday and Sunday walks, remembered him as one whose 'readiness to help, and his delight in children and animals were a part of his nature'. Hilda Wood said, 'For me it is the end of what is now a long and very happy friendship with a very dear and remarkable man.'

When the Trustees of the Aldworth Foundation met, the chairman said that Mr Willis's 'quick sympathy and warm enthusiasm for young people seeking to pursue education had always prompted him to the swift application of the Trust's funds in the service of education and social need.' Dudley Keep remembers both Russell Howard and George Willis as the two most outstanding personalities of the time.

Neither my wife nor I was able to attend the funeral but we were anxious to make a contribution towards the memorial which we took for granted would be set up. Perhaps we were acting prematurely, but when we found no one else had opened a fund, I and other members of the Workers Educational Association took on the job ourselves. There was a good response to our letter which we published in the *Basingstoke Gazette*, with replies coming from a wide area. Nearly everyone sent a letter with their donation, telling me of their personal memories or paying their own tribute. Fortunately I kept the file, or I would not have been able to quote from these letters, as I have done throughout the previous chapters.

The amount needed for a plaque to be mounted in the museum, together with a photograph of Mr Willis, the one I had taken of him in the museum, standing in front of a case full of clocks, was soon received. Our committee considered whether the appeal should be repeated to raise enough to do more than what we felt was the minimum. One suggestion put forward was to establish scholarships in memory of Mr Willis at the schools where he had been a governor, and had himself regularly given prizes. Then John Sweetman, who had first involved me with the WEA, suggested a public clock for the new town centre. Opinions differed. Personally I thought the idea of a clock which everyone could see and which would be a permanent memorial to Mr Willis was the best. It would have to be something splendid and peculiar to Basingstoke. It would have required a great deal more fundraising. I am sure this could have been done but the proposal also required the blessing of the Council. The Town Clerk was also enthusiastic. He put the idea to a committee meeting one evening but it was turned down. I was reminded of Mr Willis's experience with a Council committee when he proposed building a public park.

The plaque was unveiled, on 8 June 1972 at the opening of the museum's new horological gallery, by John Shields who had been headmaster of Queen Mary's School from 1947 to 1957. He spoke of Mr Willis's remarkable talents, and said that he could have succeeded in any field of activity that he chose to take up. The plaque was moved when in 1983 the museum was moved from the old Mechanics' Institute building to the Town Hall.

It is fixed to the wall beside the staircase which Mr Willis climbed to go the luncheon which followed the Freeman ceremony. The photograph, now in a colour version, and not the original black and white copy, is exhibited in the horological section.

More than nine months have gone by since I spoke to the Basingstoke Rotary Club and first realised how much there might be to find out about Mr Willis. The amount of information Margaret and I have gathered has far exceeded our expectations. We believe we have a better knowledge and understanding of Mr Willis, but he hasn't changed. Our greater knowledge has only confirmed that the person we met so infrequently more than thirty years ago was worthy of all the tributes which different generations paid him.

Endowed by birth with remarkable intelligence, raised by parents who held strong religious convictions, Mr Willis spent his talents in service to his family and to his native town. From his early twenties to his eighties he kept the family business going to support his mother, and help his sisters. He served the town as councillor and alderman for thirty-seven years. During those years he never sought personal gain nor the advancement of a political party or faction. He helped to direct the town's charities, first serving as an overseer of the poor in 1913, and then on the board of the town's charity committees, mostly as chairman, from his time as mayor in 1923–24 to his death. He believed passionately in education. He saw this as a primary role of the museum he founded. He served on the governing boards of Basingstoke's schools for as long as he served the charities. He was as willing to talk to a single young person as he was to address the whole school at an annual prize-giving ceremony. In the articles he wrote and the talks he gave he displayed a mastery of the English language.

His contemporaries recognised his merits, but fame did not affect him. He remained always modest, both in personality and in life-style. He had a delightful sense of humour which, perhaps, his reserved nature did not always reveal. He was generous both in praise of others, and the help he gave to those in need. I cannot do better than leave the last words to John Shields.

'I admired George Willis as much as I have admired anyone.'

For George Willis

Expert in time! Who better knew than he
The worth of every fleeting second's pace,
Or squandered precious hours more lavishly
For the common good and for his native place?
Past times he loved, and cared for times to be.
The secrets of the ageless rocks he knew,
And antique lore, and Nature's mystery
Yet welcomed change and ever wiser grew.
And Time loved him for lightly did she lay
A gentle finger on him, ne'er oppressed
That youthful mind. Now with the good and gay
Time-free, he shares the Dwellings of the Blest,
And in Elysium Fields he blithely goes
Putting its name to every flower that grows.

M. G. Monk
From *Basingstoke Girls' High School Magazine* 1970

Index

Ackland, Frederick   4, 17

Adams, Rev. B.   13

Adams, Stanley   55, 96

Aldworth Foundation   9, 43, 100

Allnutt, Cllr Thomas   31, 34, 37, 49

Andrews, Dr   13

Applin, Mrs Barbara   99

Archives, Exhibition of   65

Arlott, John   xiii, 17, 34, 43, 46, 58, 79, 88, 89, 90, 95

Basingstoke Girls' High School   83, 94

'Basingstoke – the story of our town'   86, 89

Basingstoke town expansion   95, 97, 98

Bates, Mrs A.S.   68

'Bible Women'   3

Binns, Mrs Barbara   55

British School   7

Broady, Maurice   85

Brown, Robert   65

Buckland, Sidney   13, 73

Buckland, Cllr William   13, 20, 36, 46

Burberry, Thomas   19. 34, 37

Burrows, Mr E.A.   67

Byerley, Rupert   86

Carey, Horace   45, 67, 80, 100

Carpenter-Turner, Mrs Barbara   91

Chadwick, Rev.   12

Chesterfield, Cllr Thomas   45, 61

Chute, Sir Charles   20, 72

Civil, Geoffrey   51

Clark, Mr G.   55

Corn Exchange   6, 19, 24

Coronation King Edward VII   19

Costello, Miss   83

Cox, Miss Mary   1

Crawford, Mr O.S.G.   32, 52, 73

Darracott's Café Royal   47

Daylight Saving Act 1916   32

Devon Café   47

Dickson, Mr and Mrs C.J.   63

Dore, Mrs Mary   81, 92

Eastrop Park   87

Ellaway, John   22, 44, 46, 56, 57, 69

Fairfield's School   8, 65

Felgate, Miss Mary   55, 94, 99

Fire at Burberrys   19

First World War   25

Fletcher, Lt. Cdr MP   38

Gage, George   9

Gerrish   20, 37

Gilkes, Mr W.   12

Goddard, Tom and Nora   62, 64, 67, 99

Gowing, Mr C.N.   82

Gregorys   10

Hampshire Field Club   23, 32, 79

Hardy, Margaret   38

Hawkes, Mr C.   66

Henry Place   xiii, 3

Hillary, Cllr Francis   36

Holbrook, Sir Arthur MP   37

Howard, Cllr Russell   70, 84, 100

Hunt, Miss Sarah Ann   2

Immanuel Church   7, 10, 17, 35

Jewell, Edwin   64

Jukes, Bernard Charles   21, 37

Jukes, Mrs Nellie (née Willis)   25, 36, 64, 98

Jukes, Rev. Brian Willis   73

Keep, Cllr Dudley   100

Kingdon, Cllr Thomas Maton   9

Kingsley, Rev. Charles   21

Knowles, John R.   35, 73

Leavey, Miss Mary Ann   2

Library, Free   46

Lodder, Frederick   2

London Street Congregational Church   31, 46, 98

Macfarlane, Miss Margaret   82

Malmesbury, Earl of   49

May, Col. John   10, 20, 34, 87

Mechanics' Institute   21, 44, 48

Michaelmas Fair   6

Millard, Canon   2, 9, 12

Monk, Robert   90

Munday, Cllr Albert   41, 46

Munich crisis   62

Musselwhite, Cllr W.H.   6, 70

National School   7, 8

Pearce, John   65

Peat, Cllr John   84

Penrith Road   23

Perkins, Miss Emily   11, 14

Pettle, Tom   35

Pheby, Cllr George   45

Pitman, Percy   90

Portal, Sir William   48

Portal, Sir Wyndham   20

Queen Mary's Old Boys' Association   43, 94

Queen Mary's School   9, 11, 42, 79

Queen Victoria's Golden Jubilee   10

Rainbow, Herbert   33, 48, 50, 69

Rigby Dale, Col.   70

Roman eagle   66

Rope, Philip 62

Rose Cottage 1, 5

Rotary Club 46, 57, 69

St Michael's Church 2

Sclater-Booth, Hon. Diana 10

Scott, Mrs Dorothy (née Willis) 64, 81

Second World War 62

Shields, John 38, 101, 102

Smith, Mary and George 82

Society of Antiquaries of London 66

South, Miss Mary Ann 1

Stanley, Mrs Diana 12, 65

Stanley, Rev. S. 46

Stokes, Eric 86

Sumner, Mr 32

Sweetman, John 101

Thorneycroft, Tom 37

Tigwell, Cllr William H. 25

Totterdown 2

Usherwood, Stephen 9, 51

Wales, Prince of 39

Wallis & Steevens 9

Wallis, Cllr Richard 8

Wallis, Cllr Richard Sterry 43

Watson, Mr F. 15

Webber, Mr W. 31, 46

Wellington, Duke of 73, 79

Weston, Cllr Edith A. 49, 51, 61, 69

White, Mr and Mrs H.M. 62

White, Rev. Gilbert 34

Williams-Freeman, Dr 32

Willis, Henry (uncle) 2

Willis, Henry senior (great-grandfather) 1

Willis, William (grandfather) 1

Willis, George William senior (father)

    trains as watchmaker   2

    at St Michael's Church   2

    marries Sarah Ann Hunt   2

    joins Immanuel Church   7, 10

    founds his own firm   4

    moves to 3, Wote Street   4

    visits Sierra Leone   13

    fixes Town Hall clock   10

    suffers stroke   16

    death   17

Willis, Mrs Sarah Ann (mother)   3, 25

Willis, George William

    birthplace   xiii, 3

    goes to British School   7

    goes to Fairfield's School   8

    wins Aldworth Foundation Scholarship   9

    joins father at work   14

    early memories of Basingstoke   6

    and Mechanics' Institute   21, 48

    takes over firm   16

    moves to Cliddesden Road   19

    and Hampshire Field Club   23, 32

    appointed Overseer of the Poor   22

    co-opted on to Council   25

    elected mayor   35

    loses position as alderman   45

    moves to Burgess Road   39

    trustee of Aldworth Foundation   43

    governor of Queen Mary's School   42

    chairman of Governors of Basingstoke Girls' High School   42

    chairman of Basingstoke Charities   43, 96

    and John Arlott   17, 34, 43, 46, 58, 79, 88

    founder member of Rotary Club   46

    founds Museum   49

re-elected to Council   56

appointed JP   58

house bombed   62

moves to Bounty Road   67

president of Basingstoke Natural History Society   82, 94, 98

Hon. Director of Museum   82

made Freeman of Basingstoke   70

elected FSA   66

loses position as alderman   83

death   100

memorial   101

Willis, Miss Ellen Mary (sister) (*see also* Jukes)   5, 11, 17, 21

Willis, Miss Edith (sister)   2, 17, 39, 74, 80, 93

Willis, Miss Dorothy (sister) (*see also* Scott)   17, 39

Willis, Ted   24

G.W. Willis & Son   18, 32, 55, 59

Winchester, Bishop of   39, 79

Wing, Rev. S.   49

Wood, Mr and Mrs A.G.   37, 39, 46, 93

Wood, Miss Hilda   65, 83, 100

Woodman, George   7, 45, 50

Workers' Educational Association   52, 85, 101

Wornham, Miss Kathleen   98

Fisher Miller Publishing provides a service for authors. We arrange editing, typesetting, printing or a complete self-publishing package, at cost but to professional standards, tailored to your requirements and your pocket. We specialise in short print runs and books which mainstream publishers find uneconomic to publish. You, the author, keep control, and you receive the profits. If you are interested in our services, please contact us at Wits End, 11 Ramsholt Close, North Waltham, Hants RG25 2DG (tel/fax 01256 397482).